Andrew R. Gottlieb, PhD

Sons Talk About Their Gay Fathers
Life Curves

More pre-publication
REVIEWS, COMMENTARIES, EVALUATIONS . . .

"**D**r. Gottlieb has done a real service by providing a framework from which to view a very important moment in the lives of those sons who have gay fathers, opening up an area hidden out of shame and fear. Here is an intimate look at the love and pain that sons experience when finding out their fathers are gay. Here also is the belief that gayness matters less than the quality of the relationship the father and son had before, during, and after the coming out.

Dr. Gottlieb also draws some conclusions, not an easy thing to do with such a small, select sample. One in particular stands out: that the secretiveness of the fathers was more harmful to the sons than the fact of their gayness. You will particularly like the chapter telling the stories of these young men. Dr. Gottlieb is a good interviewer and storyteller."

Norma P. Simon, EdD, ABPP
Director Emeritus, New Hope
Guild Training Programs;
New York City

"**S**ons Talk About Their Gay Fathers: Life Curves is an important contribution to the field of gay studies and to our understanding of how homosexuality affects families. The stories told by these young men reflect voices that have been unheard—until now—poignantly revealing the complex impact that disclosure of a father's gay identity has on his son. Profound questions are raised for both father and son—questions that shape not only the father-son relationship but affect other relationships as well. Indeed, each of the men who speak in this book shares his struggle to understand and come to terms with a 'life curve.' Dr. Gottlieb allows their stories to unfold and then sensitively illuminates the developmental, social, and familial contexts that impact the process that each of these men undertakes.

As a clinician, I found this book a helpful reminder to listen carefully to the stories clients tell us about themselves. While it is easy to discern common themes among these men, each voice is unique, just as each person's experience is unique. It is critical that we hear what our clients say without making assumptions or allowing clinical theory to impede. Dr. Gottlieb does a great service, reminding us that sensitive listening is the foundation of clinical understanding and, when needed, clinical intervention."

Douglas J. Warn, MS, CSW
Program Director,
Project Renewal Outpatient Department,
New York City

"**W**ith this book building on the accomplishment of his previous *Out of the Twilight: Fathers of Gay Men Speak*, Andrew Gottlieb has to be seen as a Livingstone of the newfangled family, bringing back the first reliable—and vivid—reports from a hitherto feared, and thus unexplored, terra incognita. Better, the reports are not just clinical but human, filled with the contradictions and doggedness of real people adjusting to real life. Best, Gottlieb has framed his subjects' stories in the largest way—not merely, or even largely, as lives affected by the gayness of a father, but lives in full. Indeed, the most surprising and welcome news from the front is that gayness has little to do with it."

Jesse Green
Author, *The Velveteen Father:
An Unexpected Journey to Parenthood*

Sons Talk About Their Gay Fathers
Life Curves

HAWORTH Gay & Lesbian Studies
John P. De Cecco, PhD
Editor in Chief

One of the Boys: Masculinity, Homophobia, and Modern Manhood by David Plummer

Homosexual Rites of Passage: A Road to Visibility and Validation by Marie Mohler

Male Lust: Pleasure, Power, and Transformation edited by Kerwin Kay, Jill Nagle, and Baruch Gould

Tricks and Treats: Sex Workers Write About Their Clients edited by Matt Bernstein Sycamore

A Sea of Stories: The Shaping Power of Narrative in Gay and Lesbian Cultures—A Festschrift for John P. De Cecco edited by Sonya Jones

Out of the Twilight: Fathers of Gay Men Speak by Andrew R. Gottlieb

The Mentor: A Memoir of Friendship and Gay Identity by Jay Quinn

Male to Male: Sexual Feeling Across the Boundaries of Identity by Edward J. Tejirian

Straight Talk About Gays in the Workplace, Second Edition by Liz Winfeld and Susan Spielman

The Bear Book II: Further Readings in the History and Evolution of a Gay Male Subculture edited by Les Wright

Gay Men at Midlife: Age Before Beauty by Alan L. Ellis

Being Gay and Lesbian in a Catholic High School: Beyond the Uniform by Michael Maher

Finding a Lover for Life: A Gay Man's Guide to Finding a Lasting Relationship by David Price

The Man Who Was a Woman and Other Queer Tales from Hindu Lore by Devdutt Pattanaik

How Homophobia Hurts Children: Nurturing Diversity at Home, at School, and in the Community by Jean M. Baker

The Harvey Milk Institute Guide to Lesbian, Gay, Bisexual, Transgender, and Queer Internet Research edited by Alan Ellis, Liz Highleyman, Kevin Schaub, and Melissa White

Stories of Gay and Lesbian Immigration: Together Forever? by John Hart

From Drags to Riches: The Untold Story of Charles Pierce by John Wallraff

Lyton Strachey and the Search for Modern Sexual Identity: The Last Eminent Victorian by Julie Anne Taddeo

Before Stonewall: Activists for Gay and Lesbian Rights in Historical Context edited by Vern L Bullough.

Sons Talk About Their Gay Fathers: Life Curves by Andrew R. Gottlieb

Sons Talk About Their Gay Fathers
Life Curves

Andrew R. Gottlieb, PhD

Harrington Park Press®
An Imprint of The Haworth Press, Inc.
New York • London • Oxford

Published by

Harrington Park Press®, an imprint of The Haworth Press, Inc., 10 Alice Street, Binghamton, NY 13904-1580.

Quoted text has been excerpted from *The Boy He Left Behind* by Mark Matousek, copyright © 2000 by Mark Matousek. Used by permission of Riverhead Books, an imprint of Penguin Putnam Inc.

PUBLISHER'S NOTE:
Identities of individuals discussed in this book have been changed to protect confidentiality.

Cover design by Jennifer M. Gaska.

Library of Congress Cataloging-in-Publication Data

Gottlieb, Andrew R.
   Sons talk about their gay fathers : life curves / Andrew R. Gottlieb.
     p. cm.
   Includes bibliographical references and index.
   ISBN 1-56023-178-5 (alk. paper) — ISBN 1-56023-179-3 (softcover : alk. paper)
   1. Gay fathers—Family relationships. 2. Fathers and sons. 3. Children of gay parents—Psychology. 4. Sons—Psychology. I. Title.
HQ76.13 .G67 2003
306.874'2—dc21

                                        2002012397

To my nephew Marty,
for all that you are,
for all that you will be.

ABOUT THE AUTHOR

Andrew R. Gottlieb, PhD, is a Project Director at the National Development and Research Institutes, Inc. in New York City and a private practitioner specializing in the treatment of gay men. He has previously published in the *Clinical Social Work Journal* and is the author of *Out of the Twilight: Fathers of Gay Men Speak* (Harrington Park Press, 2000). Currently, he is editing an anthology of stories written by brothers and sisters of lesbians and gays.

Earth is round, the trinity is round, the concept of the universe is eternally round. Yet although we dine from round plates we humans set those plates on rectangular tables on rectangular floors in rectangular houses on streets and acres and miles, all square. We paint pictures in angled frames and hang them in rooms that are never globes. Does the free animal perceive his world, his human friends, as spheres? Do we contradict possibilities of endless joy by blocking out our life? Could we curve our lives?

Ned Rorem, *An Absolute Gift*

CONTENTS

Foreword

When someone discloses as gay, lesbian, or bisexual, it is not just an individual event. It is a family event. Based on estimates of married gay, lesbian, and bisexual persons, a spouse's coming out affects up to two million couples. Yet its impact has been largely overlooked. Children's voices are the least often heard. *Sons Talk About Their Gay Fathers: Life Curves* as a study is a gift to the literature, a gift to those families who have endured this crisis, and a gift to those professionals working with them.

Little has been written about sons of fathers who came out during or after marriage. Data for studies that do exist most often draw from the fathers' points of view. Rather than using reports by parents or outside observers, Dr. Gottlieb refreshingly explores the perspectives of the sons, the most reliable source for uncovering what this experience means. He brings us a range of stories as well as a psychological lens through which to view them. His narratives succinctly capture the complexity of the sons' experience, revealing interlocking components of their discovery and their handling of their fathers' homosexuality.

The significance of this study lies in its comprehensive, detailed picture of sons and gay fathers as they develop their separate self-images as well as the images of their father-son relationships over time. Painful, sensitive, often triumphant—the stories and analysis of their thoughts, perceptions, and feelings afford a multidimensional, longitudinal viewing. Step by step, we follow the complicated dance of these sons and fathers as they develop and define their connection. How the fathers perceived, revealed, and expressed their homosexuality and how their sons dealt with their fathers' sexual orientation and postdisclosure lives as gay men are significant subjects, but in the end the fact that they were gay remains only one small part of their individual and collective histories.

The importance of listening to the subjects under study in order to comprehend such a complex phenomenon cannot be underestimated, a lesson I learned well while writing my own book, *The Other Side of the Closet: The Coming-Out Crisis for Straight Spouses and Families* (1994). The stories told to me by husbands, wives, and children revealed common concerns and individual meanings that the disclosure held for each of them. Until identified and acknowledged, these issues often remain unresolved and festering. For the heterosexual spouse, a partner's sexual orientation was not as painful an issue as the loss of trust, the sense of sexual rejection, the fear that the marital relationship might end, and the sense of disorientation, as assumptions upon which their belief system was built were negated. For the children, the parent's gayness threw into question their fears of peer rejection and an uncertainty about what the future held for them.

My research revealed the uneven nature of how families deal with disclosure. First, the gay, lesbian, or bisexual spouse struggles to come to terms with same-sex attractions. Next, upon disclosure, the heterosexual spouse tries to figure out what the new identity means individually and for the couple together. Finally, when the children find out, they try to put the new information into some understandable context as they cope with just growing up. Dealing with the disclosure proceeds at different rates for each of them.

As the family copes with these changes, the personalities, attitudes, and behaviors of the parents, siblings, and relatives affect how each of them processes the new information. Patterns of problem solving, anger, denial, secrecy, honesty, blame, and love also influence how each handles the disclosure. The family constellation, large or small, extended or nuclear, affects coping too. The larger the family, the more variables that impact its members. Children's views often differ from their parents' views. They are most concerned about having both parents be there for them and having a safe, secure, consistent, and loving home. That one of their parents is gay is not as important as the family breakup that precedes or, in the majority of cases, follows the disclosure.

As the stories in this book also show, the social context informs the perceptions and values that family members bring to bear on the issues. Prevalent attitudes in the neighborhood, social groups, place of worship, workplace, and school all play their part in how the parent comes out and how each member handles it. The more conservative the context, the more difficult the coming out is for everyone.

During the tense postdisclosure period, is it any wonder that the children remain unheard? They face a daunting task: how to understand the parent's sexual orientation and integrate it with their age-related concerns. Since the majority of couples divorce after a spouse comes out and some fathers disclose after divorcing, the children in these families also face problems typically experienced by all children of divorce, such as the division of loyalties and fear of abandonment. Although being a gay parent is yet another difference for the couple to negotiate, it is not the primary concern of most children.

Recently reviewing the research on children of divorced gay and lesbian parents (Buxton, 1999), I found my earlier impressions reinforced: children's perception of their gay or lesbian parent change over time; most children are resourceful and resilient in coping with the impact of having a nonheterosexual parent; children's main concern is how to meet the challenges of growing up; and the behaviors and home environments created by both the homosexual and heterosexual parent—not the sexual orientation of the parent—make a key difference in how children fare. The quality of parenthood and the quality of the children's relationship with the parent count most in children's eyes.

Life Curves brings new voices to express the children's experience, adding a number of valuable insights. Running through these stories is the struggle of gay fathers to break through the initial absorption with being gay and embrace the concept of being a father. Before the recent increase of gay men adopting or having children by surrogacy, being both gay *and* a parent seemed contradictory. For these fathers, questions arose such as: "Does being a dad prohibit acting on my same-sex desires? Will I lose my relationship with my children if I come out to them?" In contrast to telling a daughter, telling a son more often risks rejection, especially as a role model. Although some fathers come out to everyone in the family, some may wait longer to tell their sons. The length of time that fathers delay the disclosure usually affects how their sons react. If the disclosure comes after a long period of secret keeping, some children are angered that they were not trusted with the truth. At the same time, that truth most often clears up confusion and answers questions sons harbored about their fathers or about their parents' relationship. In contrast, some fathers never tell. Some sons hear it from someone else, depriving them of the opportunity to talk about it directly with their dads.

How fathers disclose counts too. Some provide too many details, rather than just enough to set the stage. Children are often satisfied with simple statements, such as, "I am gay. I still love you." There is sufficient time over the weeks, months, and years ahead to add more information as questions or opportunities arise.

Although coming out is pivotal in the parent's life, it is but the beginning of a long process in the child's life. The father's disclosure initiates a long trajectory for a son, perhaps going in a different direction than it might have taken had the father not come out. Rather than an epiphany about the identity of the son, a father's disclosure more often sets his son back a bit to reorient himself. Some sons yearn for a safety net. They want help to sort out their confusion or to find an outlet for their negative feelings. They are vulnerable to change. They cherish consistency.

The search for a father runs through many of these stories—the son seeking his father and the father seeking to be a father. Sons want to know, claim, and identify their father as father and, simultaneously, want validation for themselves as son—not the son of a gay dad, but rather as just a son. After disclosure, some fathers become more accessible, more approachable, more knowable. Others remain distant.

Reactions to the disclosure are as varied as the sons themselves. Although some sons appear to be accepting, many do not express initial feelings, such as fear, because of the shock or their desire not to alienate, anger, or disappoint their dads. These stories reveal many of those unspoken reactions.

Anger is common, especially if the son discovered evidence before he was told—and especially during adolescence when their own sexuality and desire for independence are emerging. Some displace their anger onto others, acting out as a way to gain control, feeling powerless to manage this situation. Sometimes the anger is projected onto the mother, as she is most available and safe. Other times, sons may direct the anger against themselves.

Sons may feel a sense of loss: loss of trust if the father had harbored the secret a long time, loss of control, loss of a sense of normalcy, and, if the parents divorce, loss of an intact family.

Changes in the postdisclosure behavior of the heterosexual parent also affect how sons process their fathers' homosexuality. Their mothers' acceptance or nonacceptance, support or anger, or understanding or blame often create situations that can help or hinder, respectively.

The sons' reactions are fluid and most dissipate over time, a transformation that Gottlieb's narratives capture nicely. At first, some sons are preoccupied with the new information about their dads. Everything the father does is interpreted as gay. But that focus shifts as these sons grow older and have more expansive social networks and begin to pursue their own interests. As autonomy develops, many no longer see themselves as the son of a gay father but rather as the son of a man who happens to be gay. Their father's sexuality becomes secondary. Some sons form friendships with their fathers and forgive them for the abuse and neglect they may have endured. Others form bonds with them not based on any particular interest or similarity. Still other sons continue a pragmatic relationship with them, valuing the bond for what it is.

After incorporating the homosexuality of their fathers into their picture of them, many expand their tolerance of difference to the world at large. Although some fathers in these stories mirror the development of their sons—integrating their gayness into their self-concept, their maleness, and their fatherhood—some fathers never reach that point, remaining as closeted as ever.

Based on my own research, a few differences between sons and daughters of gay fathers highlight the unique experience of sons. Although daughters share many of the sons' concerns, they deal with them differently. Similar to sons, they too suffer from a fear of peer rejection but often find a best friend with whom to share. Sons typically do not tell peers. They cope in isolation. As with their counterparts, daughters appear to have the most difficult time as teenagers, although they express it differently. Although they may feel angry and hurt, daughters can still empathize with their fathers' struggle.

Daughters, too, yearn for a father, but not in the same way as sons might, appearing more often to follow their fathers' wishes in order to please them, while sons may simply want to bond. Some girls engage in activities with their fathers more easily than do boys. The sexual overtones that sometimes complicate a heterosexual father-daughter relationship as the girl enters adolescence simply do not exist. Unlike boys, daughters are not mistaken to be gay—the primal fear of many young men.

The unique patterns of the sons' experience are charted in the last section of this book: early relationship with their fathers, possible suspicions that their fathers might be homosexual, the fathers' disclosure, and the impact of knowing their fathers are gay—all afford a framework that helps to structure this complex and fluid son-father dynamic. Through this lens, we see how the sons experience their lives, from childhood through adolescence to adulthood, making a fitting conclusion to a remarkable study that may lead to a greater understanding of children of gay parents and perhaps more effective ways to help them cope and mature.

Amity Pierce Buxton, PhD
Author, The Other Side of the Closet:
The Coming-Out Crisis
for Straight Spouses and Families
San Francisco, California

Preface and Acknowledgments

I conceived the idea for the present study shortly after completing *Out of the Twilight: Fathers of Gay Men Speak* (2000). What piqued my interest was the interview I did with Daniel, a gay father. He told me that he thought he had been useful to his homosexual son Charles as well as to his heterosexual son Todd, referring specifically to the attitude he thinks he strongly communicated to each of them that it was acceptable to "make mistakes" and "take chances" in life, ideas which Daniel seems to feel emanate from the fact that he is gay. Confident in his belief, I wanted to know if, in fact, his sons might feel the same way. Had his being gay been a good thing for them? Had they benefited from *his* mistakes, *his* chance taking? How would the Charleses and Todds of the world answer that? So a companion study, one exploring the ways in which sons have experienced their gay fathers, took hold of me. This book is the result.

Sons Talk About Their Gay Fathers: Life Curves is a storybook, an extended narrative moved along but not overshadowed by psychoanalytic theory. And, as do all stories, it unfolds. The "Introduction" briefly reviews more recent writings of the fathering experience as told by gay men themselves, setting the stage for Chapter 1, "Father to Child." Here I look at the father as seen through the ever-shifting eyes of his son at different phases of the life cycle, making him appear a complex, multidimensional, Janus-faced figure. Chapter 2, "The Quest for the Real Father," examines the son's responses to his father's homosexuality as captured through film, fiction, nonfiction, television, and the psychological literature. Chapter 3, "Methodology," explains the research process. Chapter 4, "The Stories," is an anthology of narratives that were constructed based on the interview material, painting an intimate portrait of each son as I saw him and as he saw himself. Chapter 5, "Findings," is a categorical analysis. Chapter 6, "Discussion," casts all the preceding material in a theoretical perspective, highlighting implications for future research and clinical practice.

I cannot emphasize enough that an undertaking such as this completely hinges on others in so many ways—those who lead you to subjects, the subjects themselves, and those who publish your work. Without them, a writer, a researcher, a clinician *has* no book. We are indebted to and reliant on those whom we have never met before, would probably have never met otherwise, and, in many cases, will never meet again. Like Blanche DuBois, we depend on the kindness of strangers.

So, in that spirit, I wish to thank those who led me to some of my subjects. In no particular order, they are Felicia Park-Rogers, Executive Director of COLAGE; Wayne Steinman of Center Kids in New York City; journalist Jesse Green; Bill Brown; and Michael Symons. I wish to acknowledge my colleagues Maurice Engler, for staging a valiant campaign to root out subjects; Kim Sarasohn, for applying her quick intelligence and editorial skills to the reading of my manuscript; Lisa Perera, my auditor, for her empathy, her warmth, and her sharp eye; Dr. Mary Ann Jones, my consultant, for her availability and willingness to consider some of my unique research dilemmas; and Dr. Amity Pierce Buxton, for writing the Foreword.

I would also like to thank my brother Paul Gottlieb, my sister-in-law Karyn Hollis, my aunt Elayne Bressler, as well as my friend Ed Musselman, for all of their continued support and understanding over the years.

Very special thanks goes out to all of the staff of The Haworth Press, beginning with John P. DeCecco, Editor in Chief, and Bill Palmer, Publications Director, for their willingness to, once again, see the possibilities in me and in this project, as well as to the administrative and editorial team, including Rebecca Browne, Jason Wint, Amy Rentner, Peg Marr, Jennifer Durgan, Anissa Harper, Dawn Krisko, Margaret Tatich, Patricia Sas, Marie Spencer, Joshua Ribakove, and my favorite Haworth pen pal, Niki Escott.

In the end, this study could not have been written without the cooperation of those brave young men who voluntarily shared their stories with me so that I could, in turn, share them with the world.

So, to all of my colleagues, friends, relatives, and contributors alike, I give a very warm and heartfelt thank you.

Introduction

Gay Fatherhood:
A Contradiction in Terms?

[Q]ueers are not fathers.

Jack
Jack

In Oscar Wilde's (1888/1991) fairy tale *The Selfish Giant,* our pro-
tagonist has been away for seven years. In his absence, the village
children have been playing in his garden. Upon his return, the giant
orders them out: "My own garden is my own garden" (n.p.), he says,
forbidding them to play there ever again. So nature rebels. The garden then became a place of eternal winter, in which "birds did not
care to sing . . . and the trees forgot to blossom." The giant could not
understand why spring would never come. Only after the children
sneak in through a hole in the wall does the garden return to life; only
then does the giant realize how selfish he has been, vowing that the
"garden shall be the children's playground for ever and ever." However, at one corner of the garden it is still winter. There stands a lonely
boy needing help. He is crying. The giant rescues him, lifting him up
into the tree. So grateful is the boy that he kisses the giant. They become friends. The boy disappears.
   One morning many years later, the giant, now aged and feeble,
looks out of his window and sees the boy standing under a tree that is
"covered with lovely white blossoms" (n.p.), an odd sight in winter.
As he approaches, the giant observes that the boy has been impaled
with nails in both his hands and feet. The giant threatens to "slay" the
perpetrator, but the boy exclaims, "these are the wounds of Love."
The giant wonders, "Who art thou?" The boy smiles and says, "You
let me play once in your garden, to-day you shall come with me to my
garden, which is Paradise." Later that afternoon, when the children

1

return, they find the giant "dead under the tree, all covered with white blossoms."

Poet, playwright, novelist, "notorious . . . for being himself" (Samuelson, Samuelson, and Gilbert, 1998), Wilde was imprisoned for two years on charges of gross indecency, stemming from his relationship with Bosie—Lord Alfred Douglas. Their relationship had absorbed Wilde, taking him away from the relationship with his wife, Constance, and their two boys. Perhaps the tale of *The Selfish Giant* reflects Wilde's ambivalence about his relationship with his sons. In the story the children seem, on one hand, to represent a symbol of life. It was only after *their* return to the garden that it began to thrive; it was only through *their* presence that the giant began to experience himself as a person capable of loving and giving. On the other hand, the boy at the end, although a symbol of everlasting life, is also a symbol of death. Perhaps the presence of children in Wilde's life kept him tied down—dead, in a way—and unable to fully devote himself exclusively to Bosie or to his own art, always guilt-ridden about leaving the children and what that might mean for his own future and for theirs.

Psychologist Don Clark (1979) wrote two letters to his children, Vicki and Andy, the last one when they were eleven and twelve years old, expressing the reasons that necessitated his being openly gay, reflecting on the possible effects this has already had and might continue to have on all of them individually and on their family as a whole. His quest to be himself, he hopes, will prove "a model" (p. 65) for his children in their quests to be *themselves* in whatever form that takes. He writes: "You must follow your path and I must follow mine and we must keep alive the love and mutual caring that makes us so eager to follow one another's progress along those paths" (pp. 73-74). Clark's hope is that being able and willing to live his life as a gay man and a gay father has provided opportunities for all of them to go beyond conformity toward finding their own individual, inevitable truths—ideas that Wilde might have thought and felt but could never have uttered to his children in quite that way. Clark (1979) surmises that his children are "glad to have a gay father" (p. 75), but how do we know that? How do his children feel? We know only what Clark hopes to be true. We do not hear from his children themselves. After Wilde's release from prison, he was not permitted to see his children again. They were raised under assumed names, reflecting the state of affairs in nineteenth-century Victorian England (Weeks, Derdeyn, and Langman, 1975). How much they understood about what was happening to their father at the time we will never know.

"[Q]ueers are not fathers" (1990, p. 21), bluntly states Jack, the main character of A. M. Homes' novel of the same name. Indeed, the seeming incongruity that has historically existed between parenthood and homosexuality, a contradiction in terms some might say, has been widely observed (Barret and Robinson, 1994; Bigner, 1999; Bigner and Bozett, 1989; Bigner and Jacobsen, 1989a,b; Bozett, 1989; Cramer, 1986; Gottman, 1989; Mager, 1977; Patterson and Chan, 1996; Riddle and Arguelles, 1981; Slater, 1995; Strommen, 1989; Voeller and Walters, 1978). Barret and Robinson (2000) and Miller (1979) draw attention to the *smoke screen myth,* the notion that one hides behind the facade of fatherhood as a way to mask gay identity and protect oneself.

The first pioneer to really consider gay fatherhood an area worthy of serious research was Frederick Bozett. Almost single-handedly he identified the unique difficulties faced by fathers with regard to the integration of a split father/gay identity (1985, 1987b, 1988a, 1990), disclosure versus nondisclosure to children (1980, 1984, 1985, 1987b, 1988a, 1990), coping strategies employed by children in handling the disclosure (1987a, 1988b), and implications for professional intervention (1984, 1985, 1987b, 1990). His contributions were groundbreaking.

More recently, there has been an upsurge of interest by gay men in the prospects and the realities of fatherhood (Allen, 2002; Karslake, 1999; Roshan, 2000; Siegel and Lowe, 1995), a natural result of recent legal and political gains. The "Gayby Boom" (Gallagher, 1995; Gierach, 2000-2001; Weinstein, 2001) is under way. It is interesting to note that many of the books currently in vogue on the gay fatherhood experience are adoption stories, each presenting a unique perspective. Following are descriptions of four of them.

Kenneth Morgen's (1995) *Getting Simon* is a heartfelt, sincerely written account of the quest to fulfill a lifelong dream, documenting the roller coaster of emotions that accompanies tragedy and triumph. Likening his story to a theatrical production—lawyers as directors, fathers and mothers as actors, courtroom as stage, judge and social workers as critics—it all had to be planned in advance and "the script be completely finished before we began rehearsal" (p. 60). As much as Morgen would have liked that, instead the players constantly changed and the script was continuously being rewritten. The dizzying number of potential mothers who revolved in and out—some disqualifying themselves; others disqualified by Morgen—were hard to keep track of. Now you have a mother; now you don't. Now you have a baby; now you don't. It was a game of hide-and-seek on a grand scale, one that he and his partner Sam could never have anticipated.

The question of surrogacy versus adoption was ultimately decided by Claire. She first volunteered as a surrogate but then became pregnant, much to the disbelief of everyone, including Claire herself. Although this did not fit into Morgen's directorial scheme, the desire to have a baby won out over deciding the particular method. Having been let down by so many for so long, being able to trust Claire fully took many months. He was always anticipating disappointment, fearing abandonment. Claire didn't make it easy to trust her, either. Her fear was Morgen's fear: there would be a change of heart and one of them would be left—her with the baby, him without one. Ultimately, that did not happen. A story of determination and courage, this is one man's fight to fulfill his dream, his life, his self, a story that culminates in "getting Simon."

An American Family (Galluccio, Galluccio, and Groff, 2001) documents the long-term love affair between Jon and Michael Galluccio. Self-described "sidewalk people" (p. 192), they decided that standing on the curb wasn't going to get them where they needed to go. Their story about stepping off that sidewalk and into the street of life begins with their decision to take in Adam, a foster child, born at three months old with a history of catastrophic medical complications: a hole in his heart, Hepatitis C, tuberculosis, HIV, and severe withdrawal from heroin, methadone, marijuana, cocaine, alcohol, and nicotine.

Along the way of miraculously nursing this medically fragile infant to health, they were also nursing the New Jersey state legal system, itself in ill health, which told them they could not adopt Adam jointly. Because Michael was the one with the job, he would have been the designated adoptive parent. Jon, the stay-at-home dad, was all but ignored, despite the work he put into caring for Adam day to day. Against the advice of everyone in both of their families, Michael and Jon challenged the system. Part of their journey ends with Adam's adoption, the adoption of another foster child, Madison, and her sister, Rosa, and with a new legal precedent in New Jersey, making it possible for unmarried couples, both heterosexual and homosexual, to adopt jointly.

But this book is not only about challenging and changing a system. It is also about challenging and changing the self. This hit home for Michael one evening as he came home after work and greeted Adam with "Hiya, Son." He was stuck by how strange that felt, using the word *son*, a word "small [but] huge":

> For a gay man to call a child "son" might seem at first like an outrageous thing to do—illegitimate somehow, as if the child squealing in my arms was not mine somehow but a rental, on loan from central casting. (p. 173)

That phrase, "Hiya, Son," was the very one Michael heard throughout his childhood from his own father as he came through the door after work and lifted him to the sky. Looking deeply into each other, he recalls: "I felt such a sense of completeness in those moments. He was strong, he was my protector. . . . I aimed to be all these things for Adam. 'Hiya, Son'" (p. 173).

There were also unexpected side trips to their journey, leading to places visited only in fantasy. Jon had also been an adopted child. He knew little of his biological history. Through the process of helping his son Adam find a place to belong, Jon was seized with a longing to know where he himself came from. Jon, the adopted child, was now Jon, the adoptive parent; but that wasn't enough. He thought it was better to know his roots no matter the outcome. Recounting his first meeting with his biological mother Nancy, he writes:

> The entire time as I stood there crying, feeling Nancy's keening, I saw in my mind's eye the brief glimpse I'd had of her face, the instant before we hugged. Framed in silky black hair, her face was full of pain, her mouth open in the beginning of her cry—and in the middle of her face were my eyes. (p. 139)

This moving book is about seeing ourselves in one another's eyes and redefining family. To be sure, it is not always about biology but about connecting through love, regardless of the circumstances and regardless of wherever and with whomever it is found.

Fast and funny, incisive and insightful, Dan Savage's (1999) *The Kid* is an exploration of one gay man's experience and one gay couple's experience confronting the open adoption bureaucracy. With razor-sharp scrutiny, Savage spares no one, including himself. The impulse to first attack, his shoot-from-the-hip, subversive style seems to clear the way for a surprising and a profound sense of identification and empathy with his subjects. Toward the end, he eloquently describes the differences between biological and adoptive parenthood, the former being "a genetic fact," the latter being "an act of will" (p. 234). Not only would it be through the "daily acts of parenthood" (p. 235) that he would prove worthy of being considered, by himself as well as by others, a father, but also, "enough time had to pass so that D. J. [his son] could recall these acts as an adult. [He] had to keep it up and stick around into D. J.'s living memory to earn [his] daddy identity" (p. 235). And through that repetition, through those daily acts of love, D. J. would eventually come to learn who those "large, moving things" (p. 235) were:

> He'd understand that he had parents, two dads, and he'd know that we were the guys who were always there for him. And then he'd call me Dad. And that was when, I thought, I'd finally start to feel like one. (p. 235)

Contrasting but complimentary, Jesse Green's (1999) *The Velveteen Father* is a warm and wise, poignant and profound journey of one gay man's transformation from childhood ("little enough to be lithe, strong enough to be heard" [p. 78]), to singlehood ("a twigless branch of the family tree" [p. 96]), to parenthood ("I . . . felt I had won a lottery, and not one for which I had even bought a ticket" [p. 194]), to selfhood (*"There comes a day, some years, when summer and the awareness of summer arrive together.* This was such a year" [p. 240]).

The house Green had constructed for himself was known, familiar, predictable. It didn't and wouldn't yet accommodate the notion and the reality of fatherhood without a great deal of reconstruction: "As a single man . . . the sturdy house I'd built was only big enough for one. It would take more than a wolf to blow it down" (pp. 143-144).

Slowly, inevitably, through the love of his partner Andy and through the love of Andy's adopted sons Erez and Lucas, whose rooms he inhabited, the house that had taken so long to construct *was* being blown down or, perhaps, deconstructed brick by brick—and not by a wolf but by himself, by Andy, by Erez, and by Lucas. Green came to realize that there could be no "middle ground" (p. 196) in these relationships. There was too much at stake. It would have to be all the way or no way at all: "Having answered the door when children knocked, I could not close it now without damage: It had swelled upon opening and never fit into its frame again" (p. 196).

Green is constructing a new house now, a *real* house, a home, one that better meets his specifications, one that includes a few more rooms for a few more selves—a gay, a Jew, a writer, a partner, *and* a father. It is no accident that Green takes his epigraph (and title) from Margery Williams' (1922/1991) children's classic, *The Velveteen Rabbit:* "Real isn't how you are made. . . . It's a thing that happens to you. When a child loves you for a long, long time, not just to play with, but REALLY loves you, then you become Real" (p. 5).

Much of the early research that emerged about biological parents who happen to be gay and the effects of that on their children was oriented around lesbian mothers (Golombok, Spencer, and Rutter, 1983; Gottman, 1989; Green, 1978; Green et al., 1986; Hoeffer, 1981; Huggins, 1989; Kirkpatrick, Smith, and Roy, 1981; Kweskin and Cook, 1982; Lewis, 1980; McCandlish, 1987; Miller, Jacobsen, and Bigner, 1981; Mucklow and Phelan, 1979; Nungesser, 1980; Pagelow, 1980; Rand, Graham, and Rawlings, 1982). Although gay fatherhood was considered by others besides Bozett a subject for research as well around this time (Bigner and Jacobsen, 1989a,b; Harris and Turner, 1986; Miller, 1979), it was a less visible phenomenon and came to light more slowly. Multiple reasons exist for that. Gottman (1989) notes two: (1) fathers, in general, "are often relegated to the shadows" in the parental hierarchy and (2) homosexual men are often perceived as being "anti-family" (p. 183). Certainly pervasive bias and discrimination keep many men in the closet, fearing loss of visitation or custody if or when the matter goes to court (Patterson and Chan, 1996). However, perhaps the real reason many gay fathers stay closeted is because of the possibility of losing the respect and the love of their children (Bigner and Bozett, 1989).

Besides the sparse research literature, anecdotal accounts either by or about gay men who biologically fathered their sons have also been few and far between (Barret and Robinson, 2000; Brager, 1989; Brammeier, 1989; Brill, 2001; Buxton, 1994; Corley, 1990; Drucker, 1998; Flotho, 1989; Klein and Schwartz, 2001; Mager, 1977). Still rare are published experiences from the child's perspective and rarer still are those stories specifically about sons whose natural fathers are gay, making this study all the more necessary.

To begin, psychology, literature, and film provide a context, a backdrop, for those critical moments in time, pivotal points in the lives of sons and their fathers when suddenly, unexpectedly, life curves. Through a developmental crisis, such as the Crisis of Sonship discussed in Chapter 1, or a situational crisis, such as the Crisis of Homosexuality discussed in Chapter 2, those truths seen only in half-lights are revealed, finally exposing us for who we really are.

Chapter 1

Father to Child

My mother says I am his son; I know not
surely. Who has known his own engendering?

Telemachus to Athena
The Odyssey

THE TRAGEDY OF SONSHIP

A lost homeless boy in Rio wants to know who his father is.

Central Station (Cohn, de Clermont-Tonnerre, and Salles, 1999) in Rio de Janeiro is portrayed in this film as a busy place. People come and go. Merchants sell their goods; photographers take pictures. Thieves abound and are routinely shot if caught stealing. Dora, a retired schoolteacher, sits in Central Station, making extra income by writing letters for the illiterate. They assume she is going to mail them. She rarely does. Instead, she takes them home and decides which ones to tear up and which ones to file away in her drawer, telling herself that she will send them whenever she gets around to it—perhaps tomorrow, perhaps one day, most likely never.

Ana and her nine-year-old son Josué approach Dora at the station one day. Ana dictates a letter to Jesus, her former lover and Josué's father, saying that although she considers him "worthless," Josué is looking forward to meeting him soon. A couple of days later, Ana and Josué approach Dora again, asking if she has sent the first letter. Dora says that she intended to do it that day. Relieved that it hasn't been sent, Ana wants to send an alternate letter, softening the language a bit and adding that mother and son can come together to visit next month when Ana will be freer to travel. A picture of Josué will be enclosed. However, Ana won't be making that trip. As she and Josué leave the station, she is hit head-on by a bus, dying instantly, leaving Josué all alone. Dora takes Josué under her wing. She encourages him to come home with her. In Dora's apartment, Josué finds the letter his mother had dictated still in Dora's open drawer. Josué is now highly suspicious of Dora with good reason. She has been unmasked.

The next morning, Dora brings him to a woman who finds adoptive families for children. What happens to the Josués of the world in Rio isn't clear, but adoption is unlikely. He may be too old to adopt. In all probability, he will be killed and his organs sold. Dora leaves him there anyway, purchasing a television set with the $1,000 she got from her sale.

However, Dora returns to where she left Josué, under the guise of having other children to sell, in order to rescue him. She quickly scouts around, finds him, and they run off together. Later at the train station, Josué is determined to go and find his father all by himself. He rejects Dora's offer to go along. She will go anyway. Josué's unending search for his father, a carpenter, a man who "can make anything out of wood," begins.

A gay man, a writer growing into middle age in New York City, wants to know who his father is.

Both an evocative memoir and an intriguing mystery, Mark Matousek's (2000) *The Boy He Left Behind* is a journey to a find the father he hardly knew. It is also a journey to find the self he hardly knew: "a fugitive in my own life, chasing something I never quite catch" (p. 13). Seamlessly interweaving past and present, Matousek paints vivid, compelling, and sympathetic portraits of his characters—main, secondary, and those in cameo roles—who have all played their parts in the drama of his life. His search to find his father, Jim, who disappeared when Mark was four years old after making an unsuccessful attempt to kidnap his son, starts as a dare from a friend. His initial facade of defensive indifference—"*Father* means nothing but absence to me; the word itself is a kind of black hole, sucking up what's familiar around it. It leaves me feeling mute and disjointed" (p. 22)—gradually shifts to take on life-altering significance.

Listening to his relatives' impressions of his father leaves him feeling defenseless, having no means and no knowledge to refute them, now wanting to hear what his father would say, to know "his side":

I try to picture a passionate loner, lost in his life, struggling to make his way in the world, tied down to a distant, difficult woman who loved someone else, supporting another man's daughters, coming to the end of his rope. I try to imagine my father not as the cartoon bad guy but as a flawed, confused human being who made a terrible mistake. (p. 88)

Identifying with what he imagines his father's plight might have been, he writes:

There were countless times when I would have abandoned this family if I could have, years when I felt trapped with these people, clawing the walls, waiting for the day I could flee. Sitting here with his enemies, I can even imagine sympathy for someone who managed to free himself—who may have saved his own life by going. (p. 88)

Naturally inquisitive, he wants answers to things no one has given him answers to. Writing gives him a strength, a voice he barely knew existed: "Words became powerful instruments, shovels for digging up secrets and holding them up to newfound light—blades for cutting through the dark, hammers for pounding tumultuous life into solid, beautiful stories" (pp. 105-106).

In *this* solid and beautiful story, clearly Matousek is trying to find the truth that unlocks the secret of who *he* is. Perhaps his HIV-positive status makes finding answers to these secrets all the more urgent. Although he never quite finds what he had originally set out for, he does find other answers along the way. He comes to realize the depth of the relationship he had with his mother Ida, who raised him, his sister, and their two half sisters, with the little she had within her—a mother who "was everything—eyes, ears, heart, joy—[his] measure of being alive in the world" (p. 231).

A teacher, a widower in Chicago, wants to know who his father is.

The film *This is My Father* (Clermont, King, and Quinn, 1999) tells the story of Kieran Johnson, "a lonely history teacher," who was told by his mother that his own father was a French merchant marine who heroically drowned at sea. His is a quest to find his father, to find himself, to find the truth. It starts during an argument with his nephew

Jack, after they accidentally discover an old photo and a book with an inscription:

> To Fiona,
>   The loveliest of all the lasses. I would love to be your man.
>
>   Kieran

Kieran shows the photograph and the words to his mother Fiona—now bedridden from a recent stroke—hoping, praying, to get some response, some clue about his father from her. None is forthcoming. She stares blankly into space. He decides to go to Ireland and find out for himself. Jack tags along.

The guesthouse in which he is staying is run by a woman who, co-incidentally, knows the intimate details of the lives of his mother and father and the fate that befell them. Their story slowly unfolds. His father, Kieran O'Day, was "a poorhouse bastard," a farmer, "an outsider," who worked for the family who took him in. Fiona Flynn lives across the way, a girl much younger than Kieran. Her mother, Widow Flynn, a woman cursed, owns the house in which Kieran and his family live. Kieran and Fiona become romantically entangled against her mother's wishes. When she discovers that her daughter and Kieran have been intimate, she threatens to have Kieran arrested and the family evicted. After Fiona agrees to go to a home for unwed mothers, Widow Flynn drops the charges against Kieran—but it is too late. Kieran hangs himself before he finds out he is no longer in trouble.

In the penultimate scene, son Kieran goes to his father's grave and in words long overdue he movingly, haltingly, and finally greets him:

> Hello, Father. I'm—I'm Kieran, your son. . . . I'm—I'm glad you're a farmer. I'm sorry the world was so harsh to you. I wish—I wish it wasn't. And I think—I think you'd make a real good father and—and I think you'd like—and I think you'd like me.

Deep down, whatever the reality, all boys want to know who their fathers are. That some never get to know firsthand is, perhaps, the Tragedy of Sonship. For those who do find out, such as Telemachus, the quest ends happily. For others, such as Oedipus, it ends tragically.

In Book One of Homer's epic *The Odyssey,* Athena, Zeus' daughter, remakes herself as Mentes, a Taphian chieftain who poses as a friend of Odysseus. She goes to visits Telemachus, Odysseus' son, to assure him that his father is safe and will return home soon. Athena observes the resemblance between them:

> You must be, by your looks, Odysseus' boy?
> The way your head is shaped, the fine eyes—yes,
> how like him!

Telemachus wonders himself:

> My mother says I am his son; I know not
> surely. Who has known his own engendering? (1963, p. 18)

As a young man, Oedipus' father, Laius, seeks refuge in the home of Pelops. A rivalry between Laius and Chrysippus, Pelops's illegitimate son, whom Pelops preferred, culminates in Laius perpetrating sexual violence against Chrysippus. In retaliation, Laius is told that he will be killed by his *own* son. To prevent this, Laius has Oedipus' ankles pierced and his feet bound at birth and orders that he be taken into the wilderness and left to die. Yet this is not to be. A shepherd's pity results in Oedipus' eventual deliverance to King Polybus and Queen Merope of Corinth, who raise him as their own.

Years later, Oedipus speaks with the oracle at Delphi, who tells him that he will kill his father and marry his mother. Thinking that the king and queen are his biological parents, he leaves home to escape his destiny. Ross (1982) suggests that Oedipus leaves home for another reason: having heard hints that the king and queen are not his biological parents, he leaves in search of his origins.

At the crossroads, Laius and Oedipus, true father and son, finally meet. A confrontation ensues between them. Oedipus, who does not know this man is his father, kills him. When the truth is finally uncovered years later, Oedipus blinds himself for not seeing who the man was and for the crime he committed against him:

> O God! It has all come true. Light, let this be
> the last time I see you. I stand revealed—born in

shame, married in shame, an unnatural murderer.
(Sophocles, 1959, p. 89)

THE FATHER: A JANUS-FACED FIGURE

Although many of Freud's writings portray the father as a threaten-ing, punishing, and imposing autocrat, all too ready to impose moral authority (1909/1977, 1916-1917/1977, 1918/1959)—the Oedipal father—at other times he emerges an admired man worthy of identifi-cation (1921/1971, 1923/1962, 1925/1959) and love (1909/1977); a man of godlike proportions (1927/1961), a protector (1927/1961, 1933/1965)—the pre-Oedipal father. Throughout a boy's develop-ment, the images he projects onto his father and the experiences he has of his father are kaleidoscopic, ever shifting. In Roman mythol-ogy, Janus is the god of gates and doors, beginnings and endings, rep-resented by a double face, each looking in the opposite direction. To the son, his father is a complex, multilayered, Janus-faced figure. He has many dimensions. He looks in different directions at different times. From infancy to adulthood, that complexity is captured, in brief, by way of the following excerpts.

> I ride the air with Daddy. . . .
> We enter a place where people and things move every which way. Each planet or moon or comet is on its own course, headed to an unknown place. And each moves at its own speed and in its own time. . . .
> We stop and settle. . . .
> The music moves around us, going from person to person. Daddy takes up the music. It vibrates against my back. He lets it go, and it floats away somewhere else. . . .
> I am rising and falling on the easy tide of his breathing. . . .
>
> Joey, four and one-half months old
> (Stern, 1990, p. 73)

Goethe's poem "Erlkönig" (1786/1957) tells the plight of a tiny boy who implores his father to save him from the threat of the

Erlking as they ride together through the night. However, the father is oblivious to the threat, so he cannot help his son:

> My son, why are you scared and hiding your face?
> Father, can't you see the Erlking, the Erlking
> with crown and robe?
> My son, it is a wisp of cloud.

Later, with more desperation:

> Father, father, can't you hear what the Erlking
> whispers and promises me?
> Hush, don't fret, my son, it is the wind
> rustling in the dry leaves.

Finally:

> The father is terrified, he rides fast,
> he holds the groaning child in his arms,
> it is all he can do to reach the farm;
> in his arms the child was dead. (pp. 214-215)

Five-year-old *Little Hans* (Freud, 1909/1977) tells his father, *"You know everything; I didn't know anything"* (p. 250). As a small boy looking back, Sherwood Anderson (1969) recalls, "I wasn't really the son of my father. There was a mysterious man somewhere in the world, a very dignified quite wonderful man who was really my father" (p. 82). In the famous *Letter to His Father,* written at age thirty-six, Franz Kafka (1919/1966) painfully and vividly remembers his experience as a youth:

> There was I, skinny, weakly, slight; you strong, tall, broad. Even inside the hut I felt a miserable specimen, and what's more, not only in your eyes but in the eyes of the whole world, for you were for me the measure of all things. (p. 19)

Jean-Paul Sartre (1964) wrote:

> A father would have weighted me with a certain stable obstinacy. Making his moods my principles, his ignorance my knowledge, his disappointments my pride, his quirks my law, he would have inhabited me. That respectable tenant would have given me self-respect, and on that respect I would have based my right to live. (p. 87)

Instead, he felt this:

> Worldly possessions reflect to their owner what he is; they taught me what I was not. I *was not* substantial or permanent, I *was not* the future continuer of my father's work, I *was not* necessary to the production of steel. In short, I had no soul. (p. 88)

Longing for a father's blessing is best expressed by Stephen Dedalus as he bids farewell forever to his boyhood in the last line of Joyce's (1916/1976) *A Portrait of the Artist as a Young Man:* "Old father, old artificer, stand me now and ever in good stead" (p. 253).

Combining a need for adventure with a need to find his seafaring father Johansson who abandoned him in childhood, eighteen-year-old Ingemar joins the Swedish marine. Coming face to face with him after four years, he realizes the quest to find out who his father really is eludes him:

> Johansson disappears in a dozen Tuborg beers a day with about twenty standard phrases keeping all real emotion at bay. Johansson is armored, in a bunker, formed by the grim grind of ordinary days. Inside those steel-coated, thick walls, perhaps there once lived a crying child, scratching the walls in vain because it was not allowed to grow up. It had no words. Now it has died. And I have no way of forcing my way inside to see how it once looked. (Jönsson, 1991, p. 162)

On the threshold of manhood, *Hamlet* (Shakespeare, 1988) describes his father like this:

See what a grace was seated on this brow:
Hyperion's curls, the front of Jove himself,
An eye like Mars to threaten and command,
A station like the herald Mercury
New-lighted on a heaven-kissing hill—
A combination and a form indeed
Where every god did seem to set his seal
To give the world assurance of a man. (3.4.56-63)

In *Death of a Salesman* (Miller, 1958), Biff deflates his father, Willy, with: "Pop! I'm a dime a dozen, and so are you!" Willy snaps back, trying to salvage whatever he has left of himself: "I am not a dime a dozen! I am Willy Loman, and you are Biff Loman!" (p. 132). In *All My Sons* (Miller, 1947/2000), Chris tells his father: "I know you're no worse than most men but I thought you were better. I never saw you as a man. I saw you as my father" (p. 82).

THE CRISIS OF SONSHIP:
THE FATHER THROUGH THE LIFE CYCLE

As I have previously observed (Gottlieb, 2000), crisis takes many forms. It can be developmental or situational, regressive or progressive. It presents *danger;* it presents *opportunity.* This chapter looks at developmental crisis, those critical moments in time when the son comes face to face with his father as they move together through life. It is what I call the Crisis of Sonship.

In the very beginning is mother. But in the beginning is also father. A child's recognition of him occurs only shortly after the recognition of her, according to Abelin (1971). He notes that the infant's relationship with both mother and father begins in what Mahler, Pine, and Bergman (1975) term *symbiosis* (from one to four months) in the form of the smiling response. Recognition and attachment progress over the next four to eight months during *hatching* or *differentiation,* but it is during the *practicing* period (from eight to fifteen months), a time when the child literally practices or tests out its independence—that a "turning toward the father" (Abelin, 1971, p. 246) becomes increasingly obvious. He represents otherness, excitement, novelty. He eases the fears and anxieties that naturally come with exploring the ever-widening world.

During *rapprochement* (from fifteen to twenty-four months), a time when there is a tension between the need for independence and the need for closeness, *early triangulation* occurs, a precursor to the Oedipal situation proper, in which the toddler cannot decide whom to relate to—mother or father—while both are present simultaneously in the surround (Prall, 1978). Early triangulation concludes with the boy's identification with his father and a capacity to form a mental image of the self (Abelin, 1975). There is less discrepancy between the image the child holds *of* and the relationship he has *with* the father since the father has been a figure imbued with less ambivalence than the mother has been (Mahler and Gosliner, 1955). Certainly the whole of the *separation-individuation process* (Mahler, Pine, and Bergman, 1975) is dependent on both mother *and* father. The mother represents the safe and familiar world inside—the world the toddler must ultimately leave; the father represents the exciting and unfamiliar world outside—the world the toddler must eventually enter.

Blos (1985) suggests that in the boy's efforts to disengage from the mother a *secondary symbiotic state* (p. 13) is created, characterized by a dependency on and a closeness with the father, who now becomes primary as the boy seeks, through identification, to consolidate a sense of himself as male (Tyson, 1982) and as a subject of desire, one who acts *on* the world, not just one who is acted upon *by* the world (Benjamin, 1995). Father love is *identificatory*. A child's " 'love affair with the world' turns into a homoerotic love affair with the father, who represents the world" (p. 124). Father absence, however—physical or psychological—can result in that state of longing Herzog (1980, 1982) refers to as *father hunger*.

Ira, age twenty-eight months, the youngest of three boys, was brought to therapy after experiencing nightmares in which he would come running out of his bedroom "as though being chased" (Herzog, 1982, p. 164). Neither his mother nor the housekeeper could soothe him. His father had moved out of the home four months prior after falling in love with another woman. Ira saw him only on the weekends. During one episode, Ira awakened screaming: "daddy, daddy. . . . They are after me. Please don't let them hurt me" (p. 164). His father reassured him: "It's a dream Ira, do not be afraid" (p. 164).

In exploring the dream content in treatment, an image of Big Bird eating a boy's head emerged. Ira's solution to the problem was: "Get the daddy. . . . He is like the boy. He can [help] because he knows the boy. He is not a mommy" (p. 165). Ira clearly had displaced his own aggression about the loss of his father onto Big Bird. And, as with Freud's (1909/1977) *Little Hans,* a phobia resulted. Eventually, the father returned home, concerned about the effect his absence was having on his son, and then began his own therapy. Ira's symptoms subsided.

As a boy moves into the phallic phase, father-as-loving-protector now converts into father-as-fierce-competitor. In the tale *Jack and the Beanstalk,* the white cow has dried up. Jack's mother orders him to go sell it at the market. Along the way, he meets a man who gives him five beans instead. Proudly, Jack returns home only to be reprimanded by his mother, who is in disbelief that Jack could be so irresponsible. She throws the beans out the window. The next morning, Jack awakens to find a huge beanstalk growing outside: "It shoved among the clouds and went beyond" (Garner, 1992, n.p.). He begins his ascent.

At the top of the beanstalk, Jack discovers a new land. A castle is in the distance. Being hungry, Jack knocks. A woman answers, offering him food and drink, but warning him about her husband, the giant, who eats people. Jack is too hungry to care. The giant enters, smelling young flesh. She hides Jack in the oven:

> Fee! Fi! Fo! Fum!
> I smell the blood of an Englishman!
> Be he alive, or be he dead,
> I'll grind his bones to make my bread!

The wife assures the giant that it is only his breakfast he smells. After eating his meal and counting his gold, the giant falls asleep. Jack pops out of the oven, steals the bags of gold, and scurries down the beanstalk.

Jack and his mother live well enough for awhile, but when they run out of money, Jack again climbs the beanstalk and returns to the castle. The cycle is repeated. This time, Jack makes off with the hen that lays the golden eggs.

Leaving his mother for the third time, Jack returns to the castle. This time he sneaks into the kitchen and hides, and the giant's wife is unaware of his presence. The giant asks for his singing harp and, after a lullaby, he nods off. Jack comes out of hiding, grabs the harp, and heads for the door. But the harp cries, "Master! Master!" (n.p.) and wakes the giant. He chases Jack out of the castle and down the beanstalk. But Jack, quicker, speedier, gets to the bottom first, chopping the beanstalk down. The giant falls to the ground—dead.

As Bettelheim (1977) observes, this story is about the boy's move from orality, through anality, and finally to genitality. It is about the disillusionment that comes with the realization that unending emotional supplies are available and the belief in the power of one's own body. The Oedipal triangle here is between the giant, the giant's wife, and Jack. The giant's presence acts as an impingement on Jack and vice versa. Each wants the other out of the way. Jack wants to take what is not rightfully his and consequently fears retaliation by the giant. The wife's decision to hide Jack in the oven, offering him womblike protection from the dangers of the world, permits him the necessary security to develop a capacity for independence. In destroying the giant, who represents oral greed, Jack bids farewell to what is safe and known. With possession of the bags of gold and the golden eggs, both symbols of anality, he can then move toward a higher level of development symbolized by possession of the golden harp.

The period of latency is roughly divided into two stages: the first occurs between five and eight years; the second between eight and ten years (Bornstein, 1951). It is characterized by a tension between the superego and the drives, frequently manifested by the child's ambivalence, evidenced "by an alternation between obedience and rebellion" (p. 280), particularly during the first stage.

Geppetto, the woodcarver, wants a boy after his own image, but Pinocchio has other ideas. He wants his independence. After learning to walk, he quickly takes off, leaving Geppetto far behind. Eventually he returns home, not especially remorseful about the worry he has caused Geppetto. Pinocchio promises at least to "try to do things right": "I'll even go to school" (Thrasher, 1992, p. 16). However, it doesn't take long for him to be lured into the excitement and dangers of the outside world.

The good characters he meets along the way—the puppeteer who gives him the five gold coins, the Blue Fairy who gives him shelter, all the animals who try to point him in the right direction (the cricket, the parrot, the pigeon, the dolphin, the snail, the tuna)—and the bad characters—the cat, the wolf, Lampwick, the coachman, the ringmaster, the shark—all represent the good and bad parts of Pinocchio, all separate, unintegrated parts of the self. It took the consistent love of a good mother figure—the Blue Fairy—who provided understanding and acceptance when he needed it most and a father who was always beckoning and waiting for him to come home for Pinocchio to attain a fuller integration of those opposing selves and a firmer, more fluid superego, finally allowing him to become a real boy.

Adolescence demands that we emotionally disengage from our early object ties. This is no easy developmental matter as it inevitably brings up a sense of loss (Pine, 1989; Wolfenstein, 1966), sometimes leading to feeling estranged from the world and estranged from the self (Blos, 1967). It is a long road ahead. Let us now look at the preadolescent boy who wants his idealized father first and foremost as his companion and confidant (Blos, 1970).

The Yearling (Rawlings, 1938/1967) tells the moving story of Jody Baxter, a boy on the threshold of adolescence. Although he has seen much in his young life, nothing can prepare him for the most difficult thing he now has to face. Living on a farm in the backwoods of Florida, Ory and Penny Baxter had gone through many of their own crises, including the death of all their children. When Jody comes along, Ma can think only that he might go the way the others have and so maintains a sense of detachment from him. She cannot bear to love and then lose another child. But Pa sees in Jody a boy who is "wide-eyed and breathless before the miracle of bird and creature, of flower and tree, of wind and rain and sun and moon" (p. 20), a boy just like himself. Father and son become inseparable.

Pa teaches Jody everything he knows about farming, hunting, and surviving life in the backwoods, preparing him for the difficulties that will inevitably confront him in the days, months, and years ahead. On their way to find out if their hogs have been trapped and stolen by their neighbors, the Forresters, Pa is attacked by a rattlesnake. Spotting a doe ahead and struggling with all that he has, Penny shoots the deer and cuts out the liver, applying it to the snakebite in order to draw out the venom. Pa orders Jody to go to the Forresters to ask them if they will ride to town and get Doc Wilson, his last hope for survival. Before taking off, Jody hears something moving in the brush. Looking back, he spots a fawn, "[i]ts dark eyes . . . wide and wondering" (p. 148). Its mother had been taken away. It was all alone.

The next day, after it appears that Pa is going to pull through, Jody pleads with him to be allowed to go back into the woods, get the fawn, and raise it as his own. Pa agrees, unable to say no, grateful that he himself survived the night.

Much like Jody and his father, Jody and his fawn, Flag, become one. Also like Jody, Flag grew up quickly—too quickly perhaps, becoming increasingly difficult to manage. He begins to eat the crops, the family's only means of survival. Jody begs him to please be good, but it was no use. Flag was first and foremost an animal born in the wild. Putting up a fence to keep him away proved futile at best. It was too little, too late. Flag ultimately jumped over it, destroying everything, leaving the family desperate, wondering if they were going to survive at all. The time had come for a decision. Pa instructs Jody to "[t]ake the yearlin' out in the woods and tie him and shoot him" (p. 402).

In complete disbelief, Jody leaves home. He returns the next day, admitting to his father that he still cannot bring himself to do what has to be done. With no other choices left and Pa now injured, his mother must do the dirty work. Unaccustomed to using a gun, the best she can do is wound Flag. Pa begs Jody to finish the job. Jody fires back, "You went back on me. You told her to do it. . . . I hate you. I hope you die" (p. 410).

But Jody knows what must be done. He knows his father is right; he knows that this event will be the turning point in his young life; he knows that killing his yearling is like killing the yearling in himself, that boy yearning to be a man but frightened about what life holds. There is no turning back. He shoots Flag.

In their final reconciliation, Jody's father admits that he always wanted to protect him, to delay the hurt that he was bound to face in a world *full* of hurt: "I wanted you to frolic with your yearlin'. I knowed the lonesomeness he eased for you. But ever' man's lonesome. What's he to do then? . . . Why, take it for his share and go on" (p. 426). How will Jody survive without Flag? He could never love anything the way he loved him. What is he to do? Nothing but "take it for his share and go on" (p. 426).

A slow disillusionment with and a more realistic assessment of the father (Blos, 1970; Esman, 1982) combined with the son's beginning capacity to separate from him and carve out his own sense of self are evident in the film *Life with Father* (Buckner and Curtiz, 1981), a portrait of a well-to-do family in turn-of-the-century New York City. Clarence Day Jr. will be going off to Yale in the fall. He desperately wants a new suit after ruining his old one but would be happy to settle for one of his father's specifically altered for him. After momentary consideration, Clarence Sr. goes along with the idea.

Smitten by the family houseguest of the moment, the young and beautiful Mary Skinner who has accompanied their cousin Cora, Clarence Jr. wants to impress her. However, he realizes that in his father's clothes he cannot be himself. He confesses to his mother that at a party for Mary the night before

> [w]e were playing musical chairs and some girl sat down suddenly right in my lap. Well, I jumped up so fast, she almost got hurt. She was sitting on Father's trousers. Oh, Mother, I've got to have a suit of my own.

Later, even more desperate, he begs his father.

CLARENCE JR.: But I can't do anything in your clothes that you wouldn't do.

CLARENCE SR.: Well, if my old clothes make you behave yourself, I don't think you want to wear anything else.

CLARENCE JR.: Oh, no. You're you and I'm me. I want to be myself!

In late adolescence, the son's idealization of his father has now been substantially altered. Disillusionment has now been accepted (Esman, 1982). *The Great Santini* (Pratt and Carlino, 1981) gives us father and son as equal combatants, all-out Oedipal rivals (Blos, 1970). It takes us into the world of Bull Meechum, a lieutenant colonel in the Marines, a fighter pilot of the first rank, "a warrior without a war." He does not seem to be able to draw a distinction between training a troop of novice Marines ("I want you to look on me like I was, well, God. If I say something, you pretend it's coming from the burning bush.") and being head of a household. (About their move to yet another town, he tells his complaining children, "This said belly-aching will end as of fifteen-thirty hours, will not affect the morale of this squadron, henceforth. Do I make myself clear?") Bull prefers that his kids be tough, able to "chew nails" rather than eat "cotton candy" as everyone else does, insisting they "gobble up the world" before the world gobbles up them.

Central here is the relationship between Bull and his eighteen-year-old son, Ben. He needs Ben to act as a camouflage and to mirror his grandiose false self, fearful of exposing his pathetic, disintegrated true self. Ben is continually in conflict between trying to extricate himself from his father's grip and giving in to his father's need for total domination.

In a pivotal scene, Ben takes it upon himself to come to the aid of his friend, Toomer, their housekeeper's son, when he finds out that Toomer may be in danger of being hurt by a neighborhood tough out to get him. After Ben alerts his father by telephone of his intentions, and after "a direct order" from the father *not* to intervene, Ben decides to go anyway. When he gets to Toomer's house trailer, it's too late. Toomer has already been shot. He puts his body in the car and, down the road, runs into his father whose only aim is to reprimand his son for not following orders. A confrontation ensues. Ben tearfully begs his father to try to understand why he disobeyed him:

BEN: Because I was your son.

BULL: What the hell's that gotta do with it?

BEN: Because you would'a done it. Santini would'a done it.

BULL: We're not talking about me, goddamn it. We're talking about you!

BEN: Oh, sure. And I'm a Meechum. A Meechum's a thoroughbred, a winner all the way. He chews nails while the other kids eat cotton candy. He never surrenders. He never gives up.

BULL: You disobeyed a direct order!

BEN: I thought Toomer might be in trouble.

BULL: I told you he could take care of himself.

BEN: Yes, sir. That's what you told me.

After noticing Toomer in the car, Bull approaches him: "Hey, Toomer. How're you doin', sports fan?" No answer. Toomer is dead. Embarrassed, knowing he is wrong but not willing to admit it, the father looks at his son, asking him why he didn't "say something." "Nobody tells you anything, Dad," Ben says with a mixture of triumph and exasperation. At that moment, the balance of power between them has shifted, their relationship changed forever. Ben is finally free.

The adult son and his father are in flux both separately and together. As the younger man begins to assume a greater sense of self-sufficiency, the power differential inevitably shifts (Colarusso and Nemiroff, 1981; Sheehy, 1998). Although the son is less reliant on his father in some ways, he continues to need him in other ways, through support, reassurance, and love. As the father attempts to find another place for himself, he experiences an increased sense of "weakness, passivity, and helplessness in relation to another man who is important to him" (Colarusso and Nemiroff, 1981, p. 132), "his own son, his guarantor of immortality" (Sheehy, 1998, p. 36). In negotiating this transition, the adult "son makes his father feel redundant" (p. 37) just as the father made his young son feel redundant earlier in life. The tables have now turned.

Arthur Miller's play *All My Sons* (1947/2000) begins as a story about Joe Keller, a sixty-one-year-old businessman. He lives for work and family. He has a son, Chris, now thirty-two years old, who will eventually inherit the business. However, Chris is not sure he wants it, telling his father that running a factory "doesn't inspire" (p. 17) him. Joe had another son, Larry, who mysteriously disappeared about three years ago while away at war. Larry's girl, Ann, who lived next door to the Kellers in childhood, has come back for a visit. She is now Chris's girl, and he wants to ask her to marry him. She will accept. One complication: Kate Keller—Joe's wife and Chris's mother. She holds out the belief that Larry will eventually come back. In her mind, Ann is Larry's girl. For her, there can be no other truth.

While Ann is visiting the Kellers, she receives a phone call from her brother George. He has just been to visit their father, still in jail after being convicted of shipping 120 cracked cylinder heads to the Air Force, resulting in twenty-one P-40s going down three years ago during the war. George is coming to get Ann. He will not allow her to marry into the Keller clan. Joe Keller was their father's boss. George knows the truth about what happened that day in the factory—a truth that Joe has been hiding from his son for the past three years, a truth that will ultimately destroy the fabric of their family and Joe himself.

When George finally appears, a confrontation ensues between him and Chris, planting doubt in Chris's mind about the validity of his father's story about what happened at the factory, namely that Joe had fallen ill on the day that the cylinders were scheduled to be shipped out, leaving George's father responsible. Joe had been exonerated. But now, under intense scrutiny from Chris, Joe finally confesses. He admits that he knew about the cracked cylinders but was hoping that the mistake would be caught before they were installed. After that, he would have everything up and running again "and they'd let it go by" (p. 70). However, before he knew it, the planes were down and he was being arrested. He tells his son, "Chris, I did it for you, it was a chance and I took it for you" (p. 70). In his fury, Chris replies:

> For me!—I was dying every day and you were killing my boys and you did it for me? . . . What the hell are you? You're not even an animal, no animal kills his own, what are you? . . . What must I do, Jesus God, what must I do? (pp. 70-71)

In Shakespeare's (1988) *Hamlet,* Gertrude implores her son:

> Do not forever with thy vailèd lids
> Seek for thy noble father in the dust.
> Thou know'st 'tis common, all that lives must die,
> Passing through nature to eternity. (1.2.70-73)

But she is being entirely self-serving. In encouraging Hamlet to forget about his father and the fate that befell him, she tries to gloss over the part that she played in his demise. Her words fall on deaf ears. It is Hamlet's destiny to seek his father and avenge his death—just as it is every son's destiny to seek his father and want to know who he is, even if his father turns out to be gay.

Chapter 2

The Quest for the Real Father

"Daddy, are you a faggot?"

Sam
The Next Best Thing

In *How Would You Feel If Your Dad Was Gay?* (Heron and Maran, 1994), we meet Jasmine, a third grader, and her older brother, Michael, a fifth grader. They attend the same school. As Father's Day approaches, all the kids in Jasmine's class are requested by the teacher to make cards for their dads. During the course of this activity, Jasmine reveals that she has three dads—her biological father, Ron, his live-in lover, Andrew, and their mother's new husband. Jasmine sees nothing wrong with telling her class about this. In fact, she seems proud of it and a bit surprised that the other kids make fun of her for it. She wants to be able to talk about her family in the same way that other kids talk about theirs. In no time at all, the whole school knows that she and Michael have a gay father, much to Michael's embarrassment and shame. In the schoolyard, his classmates taunt him: "Faggot, faggot. . . . Your dad's a gay punk and so are you" (p. 12). Unlike his sister, Michael wants no one to know who his family is. Clearly, the two siblings are at different developmental points. Jasmine does not yet have enough social awareness to know that she may be ridiculed; Michael knows the score and wants to protect himself.

As this story reveals, children and preadolescents respond differently to having a gay father. Cognitive, social, psychological, and moral development influence the ways in which they cope (Buxton, 1994). Ordinarily, young children accept their families the way they are (Baum, 1996). The perception of having a gay parent and what that means changes slowly over time. Moving from awareness to understanding is a gradual process (Brill, 2001). The ways in which children learn how to deal with homophobia is a process as well (Drucker, 1998; Gallagher, 1995; Martin, 1993; Riddle and Arguelles, 1981; Slater, 1995), concurrent with their own growth, the growth of their peers, and changes in their environments (Benkov, 1994).

An increased sense of vulnerability can occur in pre-, early, and midadolescence, periods when difference is tolerated the least. The potential for ostracism is heightened at these times in a child's life. In later adolescence, a parent's identity becomes less of a focus. Older teenagers may be judged more on who they are themselves and less on who their parents are. For all age groups, however, the ways in which those around them handle the situation—their family, their friends, their community, and especially their gay parent and how open he or she chooses to be—greatly affects children's perceptions and their capacity to adapt (Brill, 2001). With this in mind, we will now take a closer look at the range of experiences of children, adolescents, and adults confronted by that reality as illustrated in psychology, fiction and nonfiction, film, and television.

CHILDREN'S RESPONSES

Daddy's Roommate (Willhoite, 1991), written in picture book form for young children, presents an idyllic story of a boy, perhaps six years old or so, whose parents are divorced. On the weekends, he spends time with Daddy and his roommate, Frank, who do everything as a couple: work, eat, shave, fight, even sleep together. Frank is just like a daddy. He does all the things that a good daddy would do with a son: plays with him, reads to him, and even "chases nightmares away" (n.p.). The three spend time at the ballgame, the zoo, the beach, in the yard, at the supermarket, or just at home relaxing. Mother is the one who tells their son that his father and Frank are gay. Confused at first about what that means, she explains, "Being gay is just one more kind of love. And love is the best kind of happiness."

The story portrays the situation as conflict free. Indeed, the young boy who learns that his father is gay does not have the social and intellectual awareness to really comprehend the stigma attached to it. And so the story is an attempt to capture his level of understanding, presenting it all rather neutrally without the introduction of any moral judgment.

But in the film *The Next Best Thing* (Rosenberg et al., 2000), reality intrudes. Here, Abbie and Robert are best friends. Abbie is a straight woman; Robert is a gay man. They are companions, confidants, and, because they had sex one night in a drunken stupor, they think they are on their way to becoming coparents as well.

During a New Year's party, we meet Sam, already six years old. During the festivities, as he shows his friends around his house, he is asked by one of the girls why his father doesn't sleep in his mother's room. Sam is confused and cannot answer. Another boy answers for him: "He doesn't sleep with his mother because Sam's dad is a fag." "A what?" Sam asks.

That night, as Robert helps him get ready for bed, Sam begins to wonder the same thing. "Why don't you sleep in Mommy's room? Don't you love her?" he wants to know. Caught off guard, Robert anxiously assures Sam that he *does* love Abbie, but they don't sleep together " 'cause she snores." The next morning while Abbie, Robert, and Sam are sitting around the breakfast table, Sam bluntly but innocently asks Robert, "Daddy, are you a faggot?" When questioned about what he thinks that word means, Sam says, "It's when two boys kiss and they go to the opera." Robert instructs Sam "that the word *faggot* is a mean word that mean people use when they don't want to accept people who are different from them."

Although the plot takes some unexpected twists, ultimately revealing that Robert is *not* the biological father after all, this new fact of their lives cannot erase the strong bond that has developed between them, one not based on blood and genes but on responsibility and love. Father or not, Robert's commitment to Sam remains unrelenting; Robert fights to be a part of Sam's life—a fight he finally wins in the end.

Of the twenty-three families he initially interviewed for his research, Gantz (1983) chose five of them to study over a three-year period, resulting in *Whose Child Cries*. In one of those families, Beth and Jeffrey Leonard are separated and their son Eric, age eight, alternates between them for two weeks at a time. Gantz does not isolate the gay issue per se but attempts to weave it into the narrative as just one element of their lives. This particular story seems to be more about how Beth and Jeffrey negotiate raising their son than about how Eric feels about his father's homosexuality.

Eric is portrayed as a rather anxious, quirky boy who seems as if he is trying to say the correct thing, attempting to make sense of what he hears from his father, a teacher actively involved in gay causes:

> Gay people bother straight people because straight people DON'T KNOW. They just DON'T realize what gay people are, and what life they are living. They just DON'T realize that gay people are part of our society, and actually they're sort of twice as good as regular people. (p. 154)

Later he admits:

> When I'm grown up I would probably like to be gay. . . . I would like to be very much. Because it seems to me to be a very nice life—to be gay. Sometimes it isn't, sometimes it is. . . . Straight people DON'T understand each other. And I'm like every straight person. . . . I *like* gay people but . . . I'm one of those people who likes gay people but who has all the habits and all the features of a straight person. I'm all straight, I'm just *straight*. . . . Like, I'm not gay, I'm not homosexual, I'm not a faggot, I'm not heterosexual,—I'm none of that stuff. (p. 159)

All of this seems like the confused ramblings of a boy who is being told many things by his father who himself admits, "I would be happier if Eric grew up to be gay" (p. 156). Eric is easily influenced by the messages Jeffrey sends, and seems to say whatever it takes to please his father.

Also, the narrative itself is so overrun with descriptions of the setting and details of each family member's everyday life that it tends to distract from rather than add anything to our understanding of the more important matters. Although Gantz reportedly visited "many times" (p. xix) over a three-year period with the Leonards, we do not get a sense what changes, if any, Eric made over that time—an important but missed opportunity.

Stefan Lynch's story appears in two forms—one written by Woog (1999), the other written by Lynch (2000) himself as he reflects. In the latter essay, Lynch, born in 1972, effectively conveys what it was like for him, the son of an activist gay father and a closeted lesbian mother, always living in the shadow of danger. As a teenager in Toronto, he kept his parents' identities a secret, not only because of his fear of being "ostracized" by his peers, but also because of "the threat of antigay violence" (p. 64). Police raids on gay establishments in that city escalated in the late 1970s and early 1980s. Stefan's father Michael was a major force in the counterattack.

As a child, Stefan would sometimes accompany his father as he stuck progay decals on strategic spots around town. Stefan's job was to stuff the wax backing into his pocket. The stickers read, "NO MORE SHIT! GAYS BASH BACK! The image of it, stuck there for anyone to see, still burns in my mind's eye" (p. 65). Although he was too young at the time to comprehend it all, he knew there was a fight going on—us against them. He yearned to know more.

On one of these trips, "the man in the gray coat" (p. 71) spotted them, then stalked them. As quickly as they pasted the decals on, the man peeled them off. In an alleyway, a confrontation finally erupted: "Stop putting up your fucking faggot stickers" (p. 71), he said, standing in front of Stefan and Michael, trying to intimidate them. "I am going to keep putting them up. You can keep taking them down" (p. 71), insisted Michael, holding his own. The man, with his reddish beard and his beady blue eyes, is forever imprinted on Stefan's mind—the personification of evil, "the face of the bogeyman." "I am going to keep walking" (p. 71), said Michael. And he did.

For latency-age boys such as Eric and Stefan, the response to their fathers being gay is not only shaped by a naïveté about the stigma of homosexuality (Baker, 2002; Blumenfeld, 1992; Kaufman and Raphael, 1996; Warren, 1980; Weinberg, 1973), it is also overdetermined by an identification with their father. Being more physically and emotionally dependent, a young son does not usually challenge in a way more typical of an adolescent.

ADOLESCENTS' RESPONSES

The made-for-television movie *That Certain Summer* (Levinson, Link, and Johnson, 1972) takes us into the lives of Doug Salter, a successful contractor living in San Francisco, his lover Gary, a recording engineer, and Doug's fourteen-year-old son Nick, who now lives in Los Angeles with his mother, Janet. Nick is coming for what he thinks will be a routine visit with his father. Doug and Janet have been divorced for three years, but that doesn't stop Nick from fantasizing about his parents reuniting. He probably knows that will never happen but does not really understand why—yet.

Upon meeting Gary at Doug's house, Nick immediately becomes suspicious of him. It is obvious that he is wondering who Gary really is. However, his dad isn't saying, and Nick is reading the unspoken message not to ask. Although Gary lives with Doug, he has chosen to stay with his sister until Nick returns home to Los Angeles. On a walk through the park, Doug tells Gary that Nick "may not be ready" to find out the truth about him and refuses to "force the issue," at least right now. The tension mounts.

During a party Doug throws for some of his neighbors, Nick inadvertently picks up the watch his dad took off and notices the engraving: "To Doug with Love, Gary." It is becoming clear why his father is so evasive about the reasons he will never remarry, a discussion Nick tried to have with him earlier; Nick realizes now who Gary is to his father. The next morning Nick leaves the home without warning, riding the trolley all day, frantically trying to decide what to do and where to go. He calls his mother, saying that he may decide to come home earlier but doesn't explain why. Janet panics and heads for San Francisco. In the meantime, Doug and Gary search the neighborhood. Doug berates himself for not being honest with his son and with himself:

> I should've talked to him. He's been dealing with something he doesn't understand. I didn't give him any help. How can I put him in such a position? Everything he can be as an adult I can affect and I ignored him. Too damn busy telling myself everything was so nice and normal. Any problems, push 'em off until next year. Who the hell was I kidding?

Eventually Doug, Gary, and Janet all converge at Doug's house, unsure about what to do. Nick finally returns. Doug knows that the time has come. There is no turning back. He must be true to himself, true to his son. They leave the house together.

Doug blames himself for not having the courage to say anything sooner. "I guess I was running away from myself," he admits. Summoning everything he has in him, Doug takes the plunge: "Do you know what the word 'homosexual' means?" Nick turns away from his dad, and Doug pleads with him to "keep the door open. Do you know what it means?" Tentatively, Nick says, "I think so." Doug surmises that Nick has "probably heard about it in school or in the streets":

> A lot of people, most people I guess, think it's wrong. They say it's a sickness. They say it's something that has to be cured. I don't know. I do know it isn't easy. If I had a choice, it's not something I'd pick for myself. But it's the only way I can live.

When his father explains that he and Gary "have a kind of a marriage," Nick turns away again, unable to bear it, saying, "I don't want to talk about it." But Doug *has* to talk about it, *has* to finish what he started, begging him to consider, "Does that change me so much? I'm still your father." Nick is crying. Doug tries in vain to reassure his son: "I know how you feel. You may not believe that, but I do. Nick, the hardest time I've ever had was accepting it myself. Can you at least try to understand it, please? Nick, I love you." Slowly, tearfully, Nick turns and walks away.

Perhaps Doug knows how his son feels, but the rest of us can only guess. Nick never says. Maybe *he* doesn't even know. Hurt, disappointment, shame, anger, sadness, perhaps even relief—all may play their part in the mix. No doubt a great sense of confusion prevails. It may take years to sort it all out. But if their relationship to this point is any guide, we have a sense that Nick will come out of this a stronger person for trying to face one of the most difficult things in his young life so far. For now, however, he remains unreachable.

Bozett's (1987a, 1988b) work was pivotal in opening up our understanding of the experiences of both gay fathers and their offspring. He called attention to certain strategies his subjects, ages fourteen to thirty-five, employed in order to manage exposure of their fathers' homosexuality. *Boundary control* is the first such strategy, which breaks down into three possible parts: the child's control of the father's behavior; the child's control of his or her own behavior; the child's control of others' behavior. The second strategy is *non-disclosure* or the avoidance of informing others that the father is gay. The third strategy is *disclosure,* or informing selected others, which is considered necessary in order to head off any possible negative effects that might occur if the father is discovered to be gay.

The employment of these strategies is determined by a number of other influencing factors: (1) *mutuality,* or the degree to which the child identifies with the father in his difference; (2) *obtrusiveness,* or the degree to which the father's behavior makes him identifiably gay; (3) the *age* of the child; and (4) the *living arrangements,* that is, whether the child resides with the father or with another caretaker (1987a, pp. 40-45).

The purpose of all of these strategies is to avoid *identity contamination* (1987a, p. 41), that is, to avoid having others think that the child is gay. The fear of being perceived as gay because one's father is might best be described by Goffman's (1986) concept of a shared stigma or *courtesy stigma* (pp. 30-31) or *stigma by association* (Neuberg et al., 1994). Because identity formation and peer acceptance are both so central in adolescence, dealing with a parent who is gay can challenge even a mature teenager's capacity to cope.

"Fag baby" is what the other kids in his junior high school begin to call Jack (Homes, 1990) after they find out his father, Paul, is gay, thanks to Jack's big-mouth, smart-ass sidekick, Max. Jack's parents separated then divorced when he was eleven. When he was fourteen, Paul took his son to the lake and explained to him how he had "been running away from [him]self, and a person can't do that forever" (p. 19). Jack was clueless. He had no idea what his father was trying to tell him. When he finally confesses to Jack that he and his roommate, Bob, whom Jack has known for a few years, are not just roommates but "lovers" (p. 20), Jack feels physically ill. They row to the dock and Jack starts to run. Not being "a goddamned marathon runner" (p. 20), however, he then walks—quickly—all the way home, staying in his room for the rest of the evening, wondering how in the world his "father could be queer" because, after all, "queers are not fathers" (p. 21).

Jack is angry at first, partly in response to the fact that no one ever told him what was going on: "The whole damn world knows everything and somehow I got left out" (p. 28). It is also about the stigma he may have to endure, swearing that if he himself were gay, that would be it: "I'd kill myself" (p. 30). At first, Jack has difficulties seeing his father as anything *but* gay. While in his father's apartment for dinner one night, Jack admits:

all I kept thinking about was him being gay and this being his house. Somehow everything in it was wrong or bad because it was gay, too. I didn't want to see it, know about it, or have anything to do with it. (p. 76)

This was made that much more difficult because while he hated his father, he also loved him.

But through Jack's unique capacities for humor and insight, through his acquaintance with his schoolmate and later girlfriend, Maggie, whose father is also gay, and through a family crisis he helps Max overcome, Jack begins to view his father's homosexuality as a crisis that is surmountable. His family, similar to all the other ones he knows, has their own unique problems. The celebration of Jack's sixteenth birthday is also a cause for reflection and reevaluation. He concludes all that has happened had nothing to do with him. He, his mom, his dad, and all the other people in his life, are "all separate" (p. 215). He "was Jack, all alone. Jack singular" (p. 218), a simple realization he wished he had known before. Even though he belonged to a family he was first and foremost "plain Jack, no strings attached" (p. 218).

Adolescence is a time of major developmental flux. Since the internal world of the teenager is causing changes so much so quickly, any major or minor differences in the external world may be more difficult to manage. As the literature points out (Buxton, 1994; Deevey, 1989; Miller, 1993; Schulenburg, 1985), an adolescent such as Jack, whose parent discloses, may be thrown into a crisis.

In trying to deal with the disclosure, family members typically go through a number of stages. A tension exists in the literature about how to conceptualize that process. Some theorists, such as Savin-Williams and Dube (in Baker, 2002) and DeVine (1984) in his five-stage model, emphasize adaptation and integration: (1) *subliminal awareness,* a period marked by denial of reality; (2) *impact,* when the truth comes to light and a crisis ensues; (3) *adjustment,* when attempts to bargain for change are made; (4) *resolution,* a time for acknowledging the loss; and (5) *integration,* the striving toward acceptance. Although these stages were conceptualized based on work with parents and their gay children, I think they have relevance to some children's responses to the disclosure by their gay parent as well.

Others, such as Corley (1990) in his five-stage model, liken the process to that of mourning: (1) denial; (2) bargaining; (3) anger;

(4) depression; and (5) acceptance (pp. 41-42). He adds that the pain of dealing with a family member who is gay can be "reactive" (p. 56) or short term, chronic or long term, or both. Obviously, the longer it lasts, the deeper the shame. Because each person responds to this situation in his or her own way, I think both models are useful and relevant.

Clearly when dealing with the reality of having a gay parent, many teenagers and adults experience a range of feelings in trying to come to grips with this fact of their lives. Anger, shock, surprise, fear, confusion, embarrassment, shame, even relief may all surface initially— separately or together. These may quickly dissipate or they may continue indefinitely. Mourning takes place that is similar to the process a parent may experience when dealing with a son or a daughter who comes out (Anderson, 1987; Baker, 1998; Borhek, 1979, 1993; Dew, 1995; Gottlieb, 2000; Griffin, Wirth, and Wirth, 1986; Herdt and Koff, 2000) but also differs from it. This difference lies in the presence or absence of guilt, a feeling which parents may be consumed with (Anderson, 1987), thinking they are to blame for their child's homosexuality, and one which may impede the path toward full acceptance. In general, children do not feel guilty or responsible for their parents' gayness.

The experience of loss, however—real or anticipated—*is* common to both parents and children when dealing with a gay relative. In children these losses take many forms: a loss of trust in a parent who betrayed them, a parent whom they thought they knew; a loss of a heterosexual role model for the heterosexual son, the one the son might look to for how to be a husband and how to form a more conventional family; a loss of control in being placed in the vulnerable position of dealing with separation and divorce and the conflicting loyalties that could ensue; a loss of earlier roles within the family and the necessity of taking on new roles and new responsibilities; a loss of status in the community, which may accompany family disintegration; a loss of status and stigmatization in relation to peers when the parent's homosexuality is finally made public, resulting in a sense of isolation and alienation; fear about losing or being abandoned by a father if the child is not supportive of his homosexuality; fear about or actually losing a father to AIDS; loss of certainty about one's own sexual identity, sometimes made more complicated while simultaneously becoming aware of and trying to deal with a parent who is gay.

Underneath all of these losses may be the ultimate loss, the most difficult one of all: the loss of innocence (Buxton, 1994; Deevey, 1989). Coming face to face with prejudice awakens one to the fact that the world may be a very different place than it seemed just a few years ago. However, with new understanding comes the possibility of change and growth. A danger can become an opportunity.

Jim Marshall and his wife Elaine seem to have it all in the film *Change of Heart* (Rothstein and Brown, 1998). He is a successful doctor; she is the administrative director at the ear, nose, and throat institute they began together. Jim and Elaine love each other. They also have two teenage children, Jesse and Sarah. A house in the city and a house in the country complete the idyllic portrait. All the pieces seem to fit together. One day, when Elaine is scheduling a patient for an appointment with Jim, she gets suspicious after noticing *Vista 131* written in his date book. Vista turns out to be a motel in their neighborhood; 131 is the room number. She leaves the office. Cautiously and nervously she drives to the motel, finds the room, and knocks at the door. Jim answers, dressed only in his bathrobe. A moment later, his male lover appears, draped only in his towel. Elaine is shocked and leaves the scene. When Jim gets home, she confronts him: "I don't know who you are. . . . How long has this been going on? How many? What are you?" She cannot believe what a "fool" she has been, suspended in a state of disbelief. She collapses. Life as she knows it is over.

Finding the strength to tell Jesse and Sarah is not going to be easy. After attending a support group for gay married men, his courage is summoned. After entering his son's bedroom to speak with him, Jim first acknowledges to Jesse the obvious fact that he and Elaine are having difficulties. Jesse wants to know if they are getting a divorce. Jim admits to the complexity of the problems: "I'm gay," he finally announces, trying to hold his own. Jesse laughs nervously, disbelieving his father at first: "Yeah, right. That's a good one, Dad." "It's true, Jesse. You're my son. You deserve to know. Look, if you're angry, if you're grossed out, I'll understand. But I have to know." Sensing that what his father is saying *is* true, Jesse tries to be nonchalant about it: "So you're gay, you know. No big deal. It's not against the law or anything." He abruptly gets up. Jim insists on talking more about it. Jesse has had enough. He leaves the house.

During a celebration of his son's eighteenth birthday, the first real face-to-face confrontation erupts. After Jim asks Jesse how he is, Jesse spits back, "Failing all my classes and my dad's a queer! Couldn't be better." Later, after Jim has had a few drinks, Jesse explodes again, calling his father "a jerk" for leaving the family and "disgusting" for being gay. Jim sadistically toys with him: "Are you feeling threatened because your father's a fairy? You afraid it just may rub off on you? Is that it?" Jesse bolts again. He is met in the parking lot by the police, who place him under arrest for the assault and intimidation of Trey Farber—a gay kid at school.

After the arraignment in which he pleaded not guilty and after a talk with his mother about the importance of taking responsibility, Jesse asks for a special meeting with the judge, with Trey, and with his family. He finally acknowledges what happened, that he did, in fact, assault Trey, but wants to make amends. He admits:

> I found out something about my dad and I couldn't handle it. I felt like I was gonna lose it. And I did lose it. And I took it out on Trey. And I'm sorry for that. I really am sorry.

Although the estrangement between Jim and Jesse is still palpable at the end, it is also apparent that they are beginning to find their way back to each other. They have all survived for the time being but now need to redefine and reinvent themselves and their relationships and find a more lasting, more enduring truth than they have ever known. It is a long, uncharted path ahead.

As Buxton (1994) observes, boys may be particularly secretive in relation to their father's homosexuality. They may experience it as a narcissistic injury, casting doubts in the minds of their friends (as well as in their own minds) about their maleness. Revealing details about one's family and one's inner life is not as valued among most males in a way that it might be for most females. Bonding among young men is usually forged in a different way, at least during adolescence. Schulenburg (1985) suggests that a gay father may reinforce this, relating to his son less affectionately and less openly than the ways in which he relates to his daughter, similar to his heterosexual counterpart, continuing "a long-lived legacy of 'masculinity' dependent on emotional repression" (p. 46).

The novel *Unlived Affections* (Shannon, 1995) is told entirely through the eyes of Willie, who is left to fend for himself after Grom, his grandmother, dies just before his eighteenth birthday. She raised Willie for most of his life. His mother was killed in a car accident and "[h]is father ran off and died before he was born" (p. 7), or so she said. Every time Willie would ask about him, Grom would say that he was "unfit to be a father and . . . better off dead" (p. 8), hoping to keep him quiet—for the moment and forever. Since he had nothing to go on, Willie invented a father, making him into a man who lived a life of high adventure, dying "a hero" (p. 19), images to camouflage what the truth might have been.

Before he goes off to college, Willie must auction off his grandmother's belongings. In the process, he comes across a stack of letters written to his mother over a three-year period with the name Bill Ramsey on the return address—his own name and his father's name. Would these letters finally reveal "what Grom had always refused to tell" (p. 21)? Excitedly, he beings to read, looking for clues about his father, looking for clues about himself.

Writing about his mundane life in a small Kentucky town, where he worked as an apprentice learning how to fix chairs, and about his relationships with the town folk eventually leads Bill to reveal why he left Willie's mother and the reason Grom had kept his identity a secret:

> Remember when I wrote and asked you if you'd ever felt things you didn't understand or were afraid to feel? Well, I have all my life. It's just that now, I mean—Damn. This is so scary to say out loud. I love you, you have to believe that, like a friend, my best friend, but not like a lover. I love men. I'm attracted to men. . . . (p. 47)

Confused and devastated, Willie fights this reality, wanting it not to be, but at the same time relieved to finally know the truth. Through the letters, Willie uncovers other secrets as well, sewing all the pieces of his past together like a patchwork quilt, a past that has now become his present.

Teenagers sometimes have to pay dearly for a gay father who is deeply in the closet. In the film *American Beauty* (Cohen, Jinks, and Mendes, 2000), we meet Frank Fitts—or *Colonel* Frank Fitts, U.S.

Marine Corps, as he likes to introduce himself. There is no mistaking him for anything but a real man. When two of his new neighbors, "partners" Jim and Jim, come to his home to welcome him and his family to the block, he does not quite understand their relationship at first. Being "partners," Frank wants to know what "business" they are in. That morning, as he drives his son Ricky to school, he reveals his deep contempt for them: "How come these faggots *always* have to rub it in your face? How can they be so shameless?" When Ricky tries to help him understand that it may not be a source of shame for *them,* Frank cannot see being gay as anything *but.* Wanting to avoid conflict with his father, Ricky quickly appeases him, trying to make him think that he feels the same way: "Forgive me, sir, for speaking so bluntly, but those fags make me want to puke my fucking guts out." Frank looks at his son rather suspiciously at first, not sure how to read the message, then gives him the benefit of the doubt: "Well, me too, son. Yeah, me too." A father-son moment—or so Frank needs to believe.

Later, Frank becomes suspicious of Ricky, imagining that his son is having an affair with their next-door neighbor, Lester. (In fact, Ricky is having a relationship with Jane, Lester's daughter.) During dinner one night, Ricky gets beeped on his cellular phone by Lester, who gets his marijuana supply from Ricky, who is also a drug dealer. Frank watches an exchange of money between them from the window. As Lester leans back, getting comfortable in his chair while Ricky rolls a joint, it appears from Frank's vantage point that they are having oral sex. When Ricky comes back home, Frank is camouflaged in the dark, waiting to ambush him. As he watches Ricky put the money from Lester into his bag, the attack begins:

FRANK: Where did you get that?

RICKY: My job.

FRANK: You don't lie to me. Now I saw you with him.

RICKY: You were watching me?

FRANK: What did he make you do?

RICKY: Oh, Dad, you don't really think me and Mr. Burnham . . .

FRANK: Don't you laugh at me. Now I will not sit back and watch my only son become a cocksucker.

RICKY: Jesus, what is it with you?

FRANK: Now I swear to God. I'll throw you out of this house and never look at you again!

RICKY: You mean that?

FRANK: You're damn straight I do. I'd rather you were dead than be a fuckin' faggot!

RICKY: You're right. I suck dick for money.

FRANK: Boy, don't start.

RICKY: Two thousand dollars, I'm that good.

FRANK: Get out!

RICKY: You should see me fuck. I'm the best piece of ass in three states.

FRANK: Get out! I don't ever want to see you again!

RICKY: What a sad old man you are.

FRANK: (crying) Get out.

Frank is projecting onto Ricky that part of himself he cannot face. He needs to get rid of his son because, tragically, he cannot tolerate those feelings in himself. This serves Ricky well. He would rather have his father think he is gay than to continue living under his domination. It becomes a way out for both of them.

ADULTS' RESPONSES

By adulthood, there is less of a focus on the parent's identity and more of a focus on one's own identity. Self-esteem is tied to one's accomplishments and failures and less on the accomplishments and failures of one's parents, although they can be, and frequently are, intricately intertwined. Peers are more inclined to judge someone else on who that person is, not on who his or her parent is.

In the television sitcom *Friends* (Bilsing et al., 2001), although we have been aware all along that Chandler's father is gay, we never met him on screen. As Chandler's marriage to Monica fast approaches, she tries to persuade him that inviting his dad to the ceremony would be the right thing to do. Chandler thinks otherwise. Monica is aware of her fiancé's embarrassment about his father. Chandler clarifies what his true feelings are:

> All kids are embarrassed by their parents. You'd have to come up with a whole new word for what I went through. When I was in high school, he used to come to all of my swim meets dressed as a different Hollywood starlet. You know, it's hard enough to be fourteen. You're skinny, you're wearing Speedos that your mom promised you would grow into. And you look up into the stands and there's your dad cheering you on, dressed as Carmen Miranda wearing a headdress with real fruit that he will later hand out to your friends as a healthy snack.

Whether his shame (or whatever the word for his feelings *would* be) is about his father being gay, being a drag queen, or being totally oblivious to his son's feelings, or all three, is unclear. Yet Monica feels that he should let go of all that. She argues that at least he was dedicated enough to come to see his son compete, convincing Chandler to go with her to Las Vegas to see the drag show his dad headlines. Surprised to see his son after so many years, "Helena Handbasket" excitedly accepts an invitation to their wedding.

In the premiere episode of the television series *Normal, Ohio* (Aleck, Keily, and MacKenzie, 2000), gay dad Butch comes back to his hometown from Los Angeles to attend a party for his son, Charlie, who is going off to medical school. In their first scene together, Butch is waiting for Charlie at his ex-wife's house. As Charlie comes through the door, he greets his mother, "Hi, Mom," and, after seeing his dad, "and Mom." The distance between father and son is obvious and unsettling. When Charlie says that he has to go get ready for his ballgame at school, Butch asks if he could watch him play. When Charlie says that he would rather his father *not* be there, Butch insists. Charlie finally caves in, "Fine, come. It's your life. You seem to do whatever you want anyway." It is unknown whether Charlie has feelings about his father being gay or about his choice to stay away from the family, or both.

After the game, as father and son are sitting at the bar trying to reestablish a connection, Charlie begins to verbalize his resentment about his father's absence:

CHARLIE: Look, you can't just show up after four years and expect everything to be the same, because it isn't.

BUTCH: Look, what do you want me to do—lie to you, lie to myself, be unhappy for the rest of my life?

CHARLIE: Hey, sometimes you just gotta take a hit for the team [repeating Butch's advice earlier about the difficulties of being a team player].

Later at the party, Butch confides to his son: "I never meant to hurt anybody, but I was miserable. Being honest isn't easy, but it beats the hell out of lying. I'm happy now, and that's all I want for you." At the end of the party, as Charlie gives a speech to his friends and relatives, he heeds his father's words about the importance of being true to himself and announces, "There is no way in hell I'm gonna be happy going to medical school. I don't wanna be a doctor." The family blames Butch for putting this idea in his head. However, Charlie feels a great weight has been lifted. With his dad as a catalyst, he is now on the road to honesty and self-discovery.

In the novel *The Lost Language of Cranes* (Leavitt, 1987), Philip's father Owen has a secret: he is gay. Up until now, he has shared that secret with no one. He was hoping never to have to. Philip *had* a secret—the same secret—but chose to disclose it to everyone, including his parents, the last ones to know. Philip's disclosure sets Owen into a tailspin. He is shocked at first, never even considering the possibility that his son might also be gay, so preoccupied was he with his own shame. What would life be like as an unattached homosexual man after a twenty-seven-year marriage? He cannot envision a future for himself without Rose—his wife, his love, his world.

Owen teaches at a local college. He is quite taken by another younger teacher, Winston. He thinks it might be an interesting idea to have Winston over for dinner, presumably under the guise of setting up his son, who has recently broken up with his boyfriend. Perhaps they will like each other. But Owen is not even sure if Winston *is* gay. Clearly, Owen wants Winston for *himself* but cannot fully acknowledge that. The only way he might be able to have him is by way of Philip.

During dinner, as Owen and Philip moon over Winston like "twin oafs from a thirties comic strip" (p. 282), Rose begins to see more clearly than ever who her husband really is. From her "vantage point, the secret agent's longed-for anonymity, that of the nearly invisible, the unnoticed, the undesired" (p. 282), her whole future was now in doubt: her son and her husband, *both* homosexuals. Where would she go? What would she tell others? Who would want her now? After dinner, Owen cautiously asks Rose how much she now realizes about him. "Everything" (p. 289), she replies.

In the final scene, Owen leaves their apartment and calls Philip, who is spending the night with his friend, Brad, asking his son to meet him. Philip takes a cab home, finding his father sleeping in the entryway looking worn and tearful. Philip is confused, trying to make his father comfortable until he is ready to talk. Owen finally confesses, "I'm a homosexual, too" (p. 314). Philip claims he is not surprised, trying to treat this new information matter of factly. At the same time Philip fights to hold back the tears, fights to hold himself together, fights to hold his father together. Owen explains that his distance as a father was partially rooted in the hope that if his son did not intimately know him, when the truth finally was exposed it wouldn't matter. But Philip's coming out had given him the strength to be himself. He cannot go back now. It is too late. He must now finally face the inevitable. His life and the lives of those he loves most will change forever.

Sometimes there are stories which defy all classes and all categories but which must be included because of their extremity—stories in which a son's response to his father's homosexuality cannot be clearly differentiated and separated out from the context of their relationship. *In My Father's Arms* (De Milly III, 1999) is such a story, an autobiographical tale of father-son incest, an interweaving of past and present, fact and fantasy, tragedy and triumph. Written alternatingly in the first and third person, it traces the gradual disintegration and reintegration of Walter, who, beginning at age three, was the love object and victim of his father, a homosexual pedophile. In prose rich in imagery and metaphor, Walter traces the abuse he had to endure at the hands of a man considered "a paragon of virtue" (p. 57), one who was well respected in his community and his church, one who hid behind an elaborately constructed false self, one who others would never have suspected of perpetrating years of unmitigated, unrelenting horrors against his own son.

To survive, Walter develops a dissociative disorder. Other selves, "other Walts—the peaceful sleeping infant, the terrified observer, the furious child-beast" (p. 43)—came into being, his only means of defense, shutting "out the world in a timeless, hypnotic blink," disappearing "in the company of serpents, long shards of glass, planets, messengers dressed in suits, and paintings that could come alive" (p. 32). His father disappears as well, losing himself in the feel of his son's "unblemished skin, soft, delicious, like syrup on a biscuit" (p. 32). Walter's rage and shame alternate with feelings of jealousy and confusion when his father molests other boys—"I'm the one joined to Dad. We are the beast" (p. 39)—and feelings of profound love for him, filling himself "with the certainty that I was not only well protected but invincible" (p. 43). Many years pass before Walter is finally able to recall the abuse sustained in childhood and come to terms with the devastating effects it has on him as a gay man. Much of the psychological treatment he seeks only perpetuates the sense of himself as "antimatter" (p. 64), as nonexistent. His therapists try to convince him that he is not gay, imploring him to sublimate whatever desires he has, cloaking his "homosexual urges beneath a heterosexual personality" (p. 62).

> My awareness was detached from my body, hovering around it like a flame on a wick. Several times a day I stopped whatever I was doing and looked into the mirror to see if I was still there. Sometimes I was surprised at how pure, almost beautiful, I appeared. Who are you? (p. 70)

Many years later, when his father is caught molesting another boy in the neighborhood—a practice that continued uninterrupted long after he ceases abusing his son—the boy's father calls Walter and threatens criminal prosecution if he does not get help. Then age seventy, it is unlikely that anything or anyone is going to be able to stop his dad. Extreme behavior calls for extreme measures; surgical castration is the only viable option. How Walter is able to help his family—his mother, his sister, and even his father—through this crisis, despite years of abuse and neglect, stands as a testament to the strength of family and the resiliency of the human spirit.

Apart from the more common literature that includes suggestions on coming out and dealing with children's responses in developmentally sensitive ways (Barret and Robinson, 2000; Bigner and Bozett, 1989; Brill, 2001; Buxton, 1994; Clark, 1978; Corley, 1990; Dunne, 1987; Gochros, 1989; Handel, 2000; Klein and Schwartz, 2001; Martin, 1993; Pollack, 1995; Saffron, 2001; Schulenburg, 1985; Vargo, 1998), some anecdotal material from or about sons who have gay fathers does exist, such as Chip's story (Barret and Robinson, 1994, 2000); Ben's story (Barret and Robinson, 2000); Elio's, Mark's, and Marshall's stories (Miller, 1993); and Adrian's story (Buxton, 1994). These stories, however, play a supporting role to the overall design of each work they appear in. In Drucker's (1998) survey of twenty-two families, only two of them include a brief reference to biological gay father-son duo.

In *What about the Children?* Saffron (1996) brings together eighteen narratives written by sons and daughters of lesbians and gay men. Josh, age twelve, is the only son with a gay father. He lives with his mother, Maree, and her partner, Hazel. His dad, Steve, is very much a bystander, a man mostly relegated to the status of sperm donor who never really assumed a central role in his son's life. At the time Josh wrote his narrative, he had not seen Steve in four years.

The wide-ranging anthology, *Out of the Ordinary: Essays on Growing up with Gay, Lesbian, and Transgender Parents* (Howey and Samuels, 2000) includes only one story—Stefan Lynch's—about what it was like growing up with a gay father, a story highlighted earlier in this chapter and previously published in somewhat different form (Woog, 1999).

In other formats, *Our House* (Spadola, 1999), a documentary, includes varied and fascinating profiles of both sons and daughters of lesbian mothers, daughters of a gay father, and five adopted children of a gay male couple, conspicuously leaving out a biologically linked gay father-son dyad. Similarly, "The Children Speak" (Pifer, 2001), aired on the television newsmagazine *20/20*, includes only stories of two sons and a daughter of lesbian mothers and biological daughters of two gay fathers. "Family Matters" (Symons, 2001), a segment on *In the Life,* highlights the story of Felicia Park-Rogers—the executive director of COLAGE, and her history growing up with a gay father who succumbed to AIDS—as well as offers other vignettes of children raised by lesbian mothers and another daughter who, at age five, lost her adoptive gay father to AIDS. Only one empirical study that I have been able to find specifically targets the gay father-son dyad (Bailey et al., 1995).

There is no question that having a gay father may seem to be a blemish on the otherwise untarnished masculinity of some. However, by way of sharing their thoughts, their feelings, and their experiences, the sons in *this* study have taken a risk and if not broken *new* ground then certainly widened the path, paving the way for others to do the same.

Chapter 3

Methodology

Life Curves is a qualitative research study. Simply stated, this means the kind of research that is more subject centered, one in which researcher assumptions and bias are suspended in the service of an active engagement with the world of the participants. Whatever beginning ideas one has must be shelved, at least temporarily, so that the story can unfold and the storyteller can be understood as fully as possible. However, I don't want to mislead you. I didn't leave myself out of the process. My thoughts, my feelings, and my sensibilities come into play too, hopefully in the service of illuminating the material and providing a framework to begin to understand the data.

I explore that data in two different ways—through *grounded theory* and *narrative*. In the former, developed by Strauss and Glaser, I compare and contrast through a *coding paradigm* (Strauss, 1987), highlighting the similarities and differences from subject to subject. The goal is to generate ideas, not to prove them. In the latter, I tell a story, presenting my subject as a whole person. Contrasting yet complimentary, they afford somewhat different viewings of the same material, a kind of two-way mirror.

In this chapter, I tell the story of the research itself. I highlight the sample, the search for subjects, the subjects themselves, trustworthiness, the interview, interviewing, location and modes, bias and impressions, and data collection and analysis.

THE SAMPLE

I use a *nonprobability purposive* sample, meaning that, in theory, I handpicked my subjects to reflect a wide range of characteristics. Although I may have chosen them, they also chose me. They availed themselves of a process they seemed to feel uniformly ambivalent about yet were ready enough to engage in. The reality was that since the subject pool seemed so limited, I took whomever I could find until I had enough—unless of course I felt a subject was inappropriate for some reason, which happened only once. On that occasion, the subject and I could not meet in person and so opted for an e-mail format. However, his writing was so incomprehensible I had to eliminate him. For the most part, if subjects were not included it was because they chose not to be, which happened on more occasions than I was expecting.

Similar to many studies of this kind, the sample is a small one. I tried to make this work in my favor. I hope my subjects emerge as people, not as statistics, as I attempt to capture a sense of what is unique about each: how they not only are the same as or different from their own fathers, but how they are the same as or different from one another.

A small sample can be a deterrent, however, in terms of legitimizing one's work (Barret and Robinson, 2000), but since the sample was small, my goal was small. It was *not* to capture the experience of all sons who have gay fathers. No study could do that. Rather, it was to look at a subset of that group until there was sufficient repetition of material—the point that Strauss (1987) calls *saturation*—and to try to make sense of what I uncovered. Although limited in scope, the data offer a beginning understanding, which is all I intended. Obviously the findings cannot be generalized too widely but hopefully hold enough weight to say something worthwhile.

THE SEARCH FOR SUBJECTS

The task of finding suitable subjects can be, and frequently is, overwhelming. I was filled with self-doubts at the beginning. How is it going to be accomplished? Where will they come from? Who are they going to be? What will their stories be like? Will I be able to make sense out of it all? Panic sets in easily.

In searching for subjects for *Out of the Twilight,* I wasted a great deal of time. My hardest efforts seemed to go nowhere—the hours spent on the street trying to recruit, thinking that face-to-face contact might help, and the hours spent contacting various agencies regardless of their particular purpose and function were mostly dead ends. I was determined this time around to conserve my energies and choose those avenues that I thought would reap the greatest rewards. Of course, there is no real way to know that. This was one reason the search took so much longer; there were other reasons as well.

I began by distributing flyers to some of the fathers in my last study, to other professionals, and to those attending my book signings. I posted notices on a few community and professional bulletin boards. I made contact with other key people in the gay community. April Martin; Wayne Steinman of Center Kids; Professor Joseph Hayden; Felicia Park-Rogers, the executive director of Children of Lesbians and Gays Everywhere (COLAGE); and journalist Jesse Green all tried to point me in the right direction. I placed notices in *Family Talk,* a publication of Center Kids, a New York City-based group dedicated to promoting gay and lesbian families, and in *Gay Parent* magazine. Joseph Hayden posted a blurb on several mailing lists: Gay Dads NYC; Gays Raising Kids; Single Gay Dads; Queer Parents NYC; and Bear Dads. Notices were included in the *COLAGE Web News.* I e-mailed many organizations under the umbrella of the Family Pride Coalition as well as contacted a now-defunct gay fathers support group. I also spoke with my neighbors, relatives, friends, and acquaintances.

Right from the beginning I was continually baffled by the lack of response. The reasons for that, I suppose, were both simple and complex. Gay parents and, by extension, their children are fewer in number, less visible, and less organized as a group than parents of gays. What had been useful in my prior study was employing, in part, a *snowball sample* (Reid and Smith, 1989, p. 179), that is, one father recruiting another. That did not happen here at all; none of my subjects knew one another. Although this turned out to be a good thing, posing more of a challenge to find a commonality of experience if one existed, it made it much more difficult to find people to speak with.

Not only was it difficult to locate subjects, it was also difficult to hold on to those with whom I made contact. Unlike *Out of the Twilight,* in which all of the subjects who volunteered followed through with every step of the process, several prospective subjects who came to my attention dropped out *prior* to the first interview, deciding, for reasons I was not made aware of, that this was not for them. One person had even gone through the initial interview but never completed the follow-up, despite eight months of me encouraging, prodding, cajoling, and practically begging him to do so. For those who eventually made it into this book, it was a struggle to get many of them to complete their part. Even though I had the same number of subjects for this study as I had for my previous one, the interviewing took me much longer—over twenty-one months.

Who was I looking for? I was hoping to find sons of various backgrounds both ethnically and religiously, sons of different ages, sons who reflected a mix of sexual orientations, sons who either lived or were raised in different parts of the country or other countries, sons who lived with their fathers currently and those who did not, and sons who found out about their fathers' homosexuality years ago versus those who found out more recently. I was also hoping to find a son whose father had died of AIDS, perhaps a gay father-gay son duo, maybe even two or more brothers who had the same gay father.

Although I wanted to find people whose views on homosexuality reflected a range of responses, from more accepting to more unaccepting, I knew that would be a difficult task. Those who feel ashamed of having a family member who is gay rarely agree to speak publicly. They are more inclined to hide, not to expose themselves.

Perhaps the most important thing was to find participants who could both tell me a story about their experience and who had the tenacity to stick with this process, despite whatever ambivalence they felt.

THE SUBJECTS

My subjects are notable for their diversity. Their ethnic backgrounds are Sicilian/Welsh/Irish/French, Cuban, Canadian, Austrian/Russian/Polish, Norwegian/Irish/English/Cherokee, Scottish/Irish/Welsh/English/German/Cherokee, English/German/Scottish/Swiss, Swedish/English, Scottish/Irish, German/English, Czech/Austro-Hungarian/German, German/English/Norwegian/French/American Indian. (It is interesting to observe that in this study and in my previous one, I could not find any African Americans to include.) Eleven of them were born in the United States and live in seven different states, mostly along the East and West Coasts, one from Alaska, and one from the Midwest. One was born in El Salvador and currently resides in England. Religiously, one is Jewish, one was born Jewish but is nonpracticing, one is Protestant, one is Jewish/Catholic, two are Catholic, two were born Catholic but are nonpracticing, one was raised Quaker and Protestant but is nonpracticing, one worships at the United Church of Christ, one is Episcopalian, and one was born Presbyterian but is nonpracticing. Their ages range from thirteen to forty-four with a mean age of twenty-nine.

Eight work in some professional capacity—two are social workers, two develop computer software, one is an interior artist, one is an office manager and musician, one is a manager for a large automobile company, and one works for a trading firm. Four are students—one is in junior high school, one is in college, one is in graduate school, and one is in medical school. Nine are heterosexual—three are married, one is engaged to be married, and five are single. Two are homosexual—one is partnered, one is not. Richard, age thirteen, says he is too young to be sure about his sexual identity.

One subject is a colleague of mine, another is a neighbor and a colleague, two came through *COLAGE Web News,* one through the national *Gaydads* mailing list, one through a posting on a community bulletin board, four through contacts with two separate gay fathers support groups (one of which is now defunct), one through journalist Jesse Green, and one through a gay families support group. Four of the subjects came to my attention by way of their fathers, six were through direct contact with the sons themselves, one came through a mother, and one by way of a sister's friend. They had all known about their fathers' homosexuality for anywhere from four months to thirty-seven years.

As expected, they tend to be accepting of their fathers' homosexuality. (My guess, too, was that those parents who served as the initial contact for me and who then suggested I contact their sons clearly knew their child's position on the matter.) Although some of them had concerns about going public, they were secure enough to follow through. Again, this poses problems about not being able to generalize the findings too widely. What about those sons who would not come forward out of a need to maintain their privacy? Because they probably have a different set of characteristics than those who are more vocal and visible, it becomes that much more important to find ways to locate and engage them. The difficulties in finding parents as research subjects who are more private or who are closeted about their homosexuality has been observed (Barret and Robinson, 2000; Harris and Turner, 1986; Riddle and Arguelles, 1981). The same difficulties hold true for their children.

I was asked why I was interviewing only biological sons. Why not include adoptive sons? Since this is a companion study to *Twilight,* and since all of the fathers I had interviewed in that one were natural parents, biology was a variable I wanted to retain. Some would argue that there is no difference between a biological son and a son raised early on by an adoptive parent—a "psychological parent," if you will—but I submit that being a biological parent, being related by flesh and blood, *is* different than being an adoptive parent. They are two separate experiences. I am not suggesting that one is better than the other or that one makes for a more committed parent. I do not believe that. My impression, however, is that there are qualitative differences between the two.

TRUSTWORTHINESS

The difficulties in establishing trust in qualitative research are compounded by the fact that the researcher *is* the research tool. Similar to a singer, an actor, or a dancer, you, as a researcher, *are* your instrument. You become the conduit through which all the data and all the impressions of the data flow (Mirvis and Louis, 1985; Taylor and Bogdan, 1984). Because of that, trustworthiness becomes that much more important. One of the ways I chose to check myself was by using an auditor. A clinical social worker by training and a trusted colleague, it was her job to read several of the interview transcripts for any hint of bias. In general, she thought I maintained an honest attempt at neutrality. However, at times, I had subtly challenged the subjects' beliefs that (1) having a gay father was not a problem for them or (2) there was more of an awareness of their fathers' homosexuality prior to disclosure than they were consciously alert to. I tried to keep these two issues in mind during the remaining interviews.

Another avenue to establish trustworthiness is through *member-checking* (Ely et al., 1991), a process in which a researcher confers with the subjects about whom one is writing. After their narratives were completed, I sent the first draft to the sons for their editing and approval. This is a process which had worked successfully for me before and which I believed would work again. There are also precedents and support for this method in the literature (Connelly and Clandinin, 1990; Mishler, 1986; Spradley, 1979).

In general, my subjects' remarks were of three main types. Besides style and word choice, they wanted to disguise the material a bit more by altering names and quotes; they wanted to soften the language so that the reality didn't seem quite so close to the bone; and they wanted to make sure that the subtlety of their feelings, the relationships within their families, the family members themselves, and their over-all situations were portrayed accurately.

Richard and Paul were perfectly content with their stories just as I wrote them. Rob wanted only to alter the name I chose for his father—not for the purpose of disguising him more but because he just didn't care for my choice. Mark never directly let me know what he thought, even after repeated attempts to contact him. (Nor, for that matter, did he complete the second set of follow-up questions.) I had to take his nonresponse as a green light to publish it. I had to assume he was happy with it the way it was.

Working with Matthew was rather perplexing, too. Even though he was highly motivated prior to the interview, he seemed to lose momentum after I submitted the draft to him. It took him three months to return his story to me so that we could continue the process. He, like Mark, never gave a formal, final nod to the story in its final version, even after repeated requests.

Noah made corrections and additions fairly quickly but then took a couple of weeks to put it in the mail. Joseph received his weeks before reading it, claiming that he had been too busy with work. After finally going over it, he told me that it hit too close to home and he was concerned about inflicting hurt and humiliation on his parents. Dredging up events long since buried and the feelings associated with those events, he thought, could only be harmful. We had to extensively rework the narrative, softening the language a bit so that it was satisfactory to him. The few follow-up questions I posed—some factual, others more emotional in content—took him almost two months to complete. He cited being too absorbed with career-related activities as the reason for the delay.

The most extreme response was Elliot's. Since we had done his interview entirely by e-mail (see Interviewing: Location and Modes), the opportunity for misunderstanding and miscommunication was obviously greater. Initially, he seemed to misconstrue my intentions, thinking that I was consciously attempting to show how his father's homosexuality and the disclosure were a destructive thing for him.

He eventually allowed his story to be published but only after he understood more about what I was doing and only after we altered the story to capture what he considered a more accurate, less dramatic portrayal of his family life. How can we make sense of all the reticence and ambivalence?

One explanation might be that whatever psychic reserve some of them had for this project rapidly depleted. After the interview, their interests seemed to have waned and they needed to move on to other things in their lives. Other priorities beckoned. On a deeper level, though, I think the issue of exposure was key. For those prospective subjects who decided against being involved at all, my guess is that this posed too much of a threat. For those participants who followed through but who needed a great deal of support, I think what sounded like an interesting project was suddenly made real. In realizing what would be involved and then finally seeing their stories on paper, the ambivalence about exposing themselves and, perhaps, exposing their fathers took over. Their shame *and* guilt were likely at the bottom of this.

THE INTERVIEW

The interview was divided into three major sections. First, I asked the subjects about their backgrounds—where they grew up, who was in their family. I asked them to describe their fathers—what sort of a person he is/was, what things did they feel are/were important to him. What was their first memory of him? Would they describe their relationship with him in the early years of their lives? Did any particular events stand out? Would they describe their relationship with him through the present? What were the best times; the worst times? Had their relationship with their fathers been the same or different than their fathers' relationships with their sibling(s)? What were the similarities and differences between themselves and their fathers?

Second, I focused on the disclosure and its effects. Did they ever think that their father might be gay? If so, when was that and what was that like for them? When did they actually find out about their father's homosexuality? Was it a gradual awakening or were they informed, and by whom? What was their immediate response? How did they handle it? How was the disclosure dealt with in terms of family and friends? What was the quality of their relationship like at that point? Do they deal with it differently now? Did their relationship change after the knowledge of their father's sexuality and, if so, how?

Third, I wanted to know if their father's homosexuality affected their feelings about themselves. Did it affect their development? Did they think there were/are any advantages and/or disadvantages to having a gay father? Did having a gay father affect them at all?

INTERVIEWING: LOCATION AND MODES

I should say something about where the in-person interviews were conducted. Three were done in my home, one interview and one follow-up were completed at my workplace, two in the homes of the subjects, and two in the homes of the subjects' relatives. The interview with Richard was a bit unusual. He had flown to the Washington, DC, area with his classmates, all of whom were on an educational trip to learn more about the government. I met him at his hotel and did the interview there. Except for the one in-person follow-up, all the others were either typed or completed by e-mail since, as I noted, many of my subjects lived elsewhere and would not be available again any time soon for in-person contact. Those took place anywhere from one week to seventeen months after the initial interview.

Shawn, Elliot, and Thomas were inaccessible but wanted to participate. Since they were not going to come to me and since I was not able to go to them, I conducted their interviews entirely by e-mail. This was not my first choice, but since I could not find enough subjects who were accessible I had to compromise. For them, it considerably lengthened the process, stretching out the initial interviews anywhere from almost two months in the case of Shawn, to over two months in the case of Elliot, to almost three months for Thomas. Many interruptions occurred—their vacations, the beginning of school for Elliot, the beginning of a new job for Thomas. Clearly, other priorities predominated at certain points along the way. They also needed a certain motivation to sit behind a computer screen and unearth memories that connected to their emotional lives. I'm sure this was not easy for them.

I do not know if mixing modes affected the findings in any way. The interview questions were basically the same. Certainly my experience with Elliot would argue against using e-mail as the primary mode of communication, although it seemed fine for the shorter follow-up questions that were mostly factual and less emotional. But if interviewer and interviewee *never* meet face to face, it can potentially be a real barrier and make it much more difficult to establish trust. Unfortunately, I was not able to find enough subjects in a reasonable amount of time, so I had to settle for a less effective way to communicate in these three situations.

BIAS AND IMPRESSIONS

As one prepares for a study such as this, having a sense of the biases one holds is key so that they can be kept at bay. This is critical—otherwise those prejudices, those things you want to hear and expect to hear, infiltrate and contaminate the process. The only thought one should have upon entering this situation is: expect the unexpected.

Having just finished *Out of the Twilight* and now writing another study on a similar theme in a similar way, I could not help but be influenced by what I had found there. One of my ideas beforehand was thinking that *identification* was going to be an important dynamic, that is, if the sons could see the similarities between themselves and their dads, if they could identify with them in some personal ways, then they might be more inclined to accept their fathers' homosexuality. This was true for the fathers in my previous study. Would it be true here? Perhaps it was, but not to the extent I had anticipated. For Eric, in fact, just the opposite occurred. The similarities he perceived between himself and his father actually created a homosexual panic. In his mind, if he was similar to his dad in so many ways, did that mean he was gay, too?

Another thought I had was that the sons might idealize their fathers in the same way that the fathers in my previous study had idealized their sons. However, it seemed obvious right from the start that these sons had a slightly more balanced perception of their fathers than the fathers in my previous study had of their sons, drawing a fuller picture of both strengths *and* weaknesses, particularly the weaknesses, in a way that my former subjects did not do. Did the fact that I am a son help them to reveal themselves more fully than they might have otherwise? As I have pointed out previously (Gottlieb, 2000), the identity of a researcher shapes and influences the stories you are told.

I became conscious of another bias during the interviewing: I was assuming that the sons were more aware of their fathers' homosexuality before the disclosure than they actually may have been. I also assumed that their fathers' homosexuality was going to be more of a problem for them at the time of disclosure than was being portrayed. It is difficult to know whether that was defensive on their part—an attempt to protect themselves, their fathers, or both—or if this was how they were really feeling. Granted, it is sometimes difficult for us to say with any real clarity what goes on retrospectively and what our exact feelings are at the time something occurs. Time either clarifies or distorts our perceptions and sometimes does both. However, the current perceptions are what count here, real or imagined. Finally, I was assuming they would tell me that their relationships at the present time were the best they had ever been in their lives. This was the case some, but not all of the time.

These assumptions highlight the unpredictability of this kind of research. One writes a book in the hopes that a story evolves and, of course, it does. It just may be different than the one you expected.

What *was* clear from the very first interview was that the sons' focus on their fathers' homosexuality played a *secondary* role to who their fathers were as people, apart from their sexuality. Other things about their fathers were far more disturbing to them than their homosexuality, at least that was what they told me. I wondered if their focus on those other dimensions was also defensive—a way to remove the emphasis from homosexuality. Or was that, again, an expression of how they really felt—that sexual orientation did not matter that much in the larger scheme of things?

One must always keep in mind that just as disclosure is a contextual act, partly determined by the character of the father and partly by his environment—the family he lives in, the community he lives in, the culture he lives in—so are the acts of receiving and dealing with the disclosure dependent on the character of the son and the environmental influences to which he is subjected. It is virtually impossible to separate all these variables.

Highlighted in some of the stories was not only the telling of the secret and how that was done but also the fallout from the secret, that is, how *not* telling shaped family life. That was something I had not expected to hear and had not thought that much about. Some of the respondents articulated these issues in a way that surprised and even dazzled me.

What did they think of me, their interviewer? Obviously the two subjects I knew already were well aware of the fact that I am gay. Two others asked me related questions. I'm sure most of them had a strong suspicion. All of them knew about my previous book and probably put two and two together. My guess is that knowledge worked in my favor since I was no stranger to the issue. Also, the fact that I already had a book published probably made me appear the "expert." I suppose that could have been intimidating as well, but I was never made aware if it was.

Elliot's situation was special. I felt that I had to come out as gay directly to him, given his initial fears that I was trying to paint his father's homosexuality as a negative thing. Having never met face to face, it was obviously more difficult for him to get a sense of who I was and what my motives could possibly be in writing a book such as this.

Certainly I brought some of my own frustrations to this whole process too. Being more accustomed to functioning as a clinician, this particular interview format seemed a bit limiting. I am used to taking my time and getting a fuller picture over many months or years. Having to cram it all in so quickly was difficult. My role as a *limited observer* (Ely et al., 1991, p. 45) was exactly that: limited—always on the outside looking in, a fly on the wall, never fully part of their lives. Although in some ways the role of a qualitative researcher is similar to the role of a clinician, the two also differ. In the former, the aim is to explore and understand; in the latter, the aim is to explore, understand, *and* resolve (Padgett, 1998). In both roles, however, the clinician or researcher only gets but so close.

DATA COLLECTION AND ANALYSIS

Unique to qualitative research is the idea that data collection and analysis proceed side by side. As one collects, one analyzes; as one analyzes, one collects. My primary collection instruments were the interviews—all conducted, recorded, and transcribed by me—and my log—a diary of sorts, containing impressions about my subjects and thoughts about preliminary findings.

In terms of the actual analysis, I conceptualized the data the same way I had in my previous book, using categories that were either the same as or similar to the ones in that study. Since in both I am studying the dynamics of disclosure, this seemed to make sense. Those categories constitute Chapter 5 and are Beginnings, Suspicions, Disclosure, and Impact. They provide an organizing framework with which to compare and contrast each son to the other. The narratives that make up Chapter 4 provide a view of each son in the context of this event and in the context of his life.

Chapter 4

The Stories

MARK

Maybe just really big things have to happen to change your whole perspective.

As a young boy, Mark was diagnosed with uveitis, a rare eye disease. This affected many parts of his life, particularly at school, where the books he used had to be on tape. Prednisone, the treatment of choice at the time, led only to the development of cataracts, further complicating his condition. Glasses and contacts proved awkward and ineffective. Finally, more recently, lenses were implanted, resulting in vision still somewhat "diminished" but nevertheless greatly improved: "I can drive. I can read." The inability to see what was there before and the ability to see more clearly what is there now have been central competing metaphors throughout Mark's life.

Geographical flux had been a predominant theme of his childhood, adolescence, and early adulthood. Now thirty-three years old and a professional in computer software development, Mark was born in Washington, DC, where his parents—John, now sixty-three, and Elizabeth, now sixty-four—met through a mutual friend. When Mark was six months old, his family moved to New York City, where they resided for the next six years. After his parents separated, Elizabeth took him and his three-year-old brother Jim to Woodstock, New York, to live. A five-year stint in California was their next stop before Mark and Jim independently decided to move back to New York City to reside with their father and his second wife. After completing high school, Mark attended a music conservatory in Connecticut but transferred after a semester to a university in upstate New York. Upon

---

All the quotations cited in the following stories are taken directly from the interview transcripts.

graduating with a degree in fine arts, he then moved back to New York City, lived briefly in Boston, then moved back to New York. For the past four years Mark and his wife have resided in a small university town north of the city. He is finished moving—for now anyway.

Many of those earlier moves were his mother's attempts "to get farther away from" his father. However, even after Elizabeth and the boys were situated, she would tend to relocate within a particular area, sometimes several times—moves within moves. This urgency to continuously shift the geographical landscape has dominated her professional choices now as well, taking her from site to site, "from place to place." Mark acknowledges that "the idea of a new start is a big thing for her."

The presence of conflict seems to dominate Mark's recollections of his parents' relationship. His mother's receiving and maintaining full custody of the children was intimately tied to her threat of exposing his father's homosexuality. He recalls that their arguing "was very scary and loud and disturbing" and something which he did not comprehend. When Mark was fifteen and wanted to live with his dad in New York City, his mother vehemently tried to stop him. In a desperate move, she told him that he had no idea who his father "really . . . was," an idea that was, in part, true. However, that was one of the reasons Mark wanted to go in the first place—to get closer to him, to "find" him. He eventually went. Brother Jim tagged behind.

"From age zero to five," Mark spent much time with his father, then a documentary filmmaker, now a journalist, who was then spending many hours at home. Their "very easy connection" was based in large part on shared interests and having "a similar brain." Trips to the zoo or to the museum would invariably stimulate discussion about animal life and history. As a young father, John was good at staging "the family trip." He enjoyed planning, organizing, and executing, trying to make it a "special event" that would be both exciting and memorable. He can still do that. On a recent vacation together to Italy with just the two of them, Mark learned a great deal about his father's side of the family and developed a greater appreciation of his own roots. Exchanging views about politics, the news, and the world around them has always been an integral part, perhaps "the strongest part of [their] relationship."

Although Mark believes that his father was available in some ways, he also observes that he was unavailable in other ways—"being there but not really being there"—a master at "hiding and defending himself," based in large part, Mark thinks, on the fact that he had to hide "a really big part of who he was" for so long. This tendency to re-flexively defend oneself is a trait that Mark clearly sees in himself as well, one that he thinks he got from his dad. Although the similarities between father and son are remarkable, there are differences to be sure. Mark observes that he is "better at connecting with people" and has a capacity to commit to a relationship in a way that his father can-not. Cognizant of what his father has been through, he credits him with "working really hard at" improving himself in this way, despite the odds.

For many years, his father's homosexuality was a subject shrouded in darkness and mystery. As a preadolescent, his mother told him about his dad having "had a relationship with a man in some way or another." He recalls that she was rather vague about it all, making him both curious—"I really wanted to ask him about it"—and shame-ful—"like I was carrying some dark secret"—resulting in a pervasive sense of confusion. Part of him wanted to understand it; the other part of him didn't. It was all too personal; it was all too much information he felt he could not absorb at the time, a "deep undercurrent" hard to name and harder to comprehend.

After moving in with his father and his second wife, Mark finally worked up the courage to ask him directly. What remains vivid in their discussion is that at the moment he approached the subject, his father immediately, urgently, got up and shut the door of the room. The sense that this was, in fact, a secret was clearer in hindsight. Al-though John did not deny he had had an affair with another man, he implied "it was something that he experimented with," but that it was in the past, an explanation that Mark "was all too happy to accept." It wasn't until eight years later that John, then age fifty-three, was ready for full disclosure, this time staged as another "one of those family events."

Present were Mark, his brother Jim, their two younger half sisters, ages ten and thirteen, John, and his second wife. Although the couple had separated a few months before this, Mark thinks that they needed to keep up the pretense of still being together until the disclosure was made, which, apparently, came as no surprise to Mark: "I mean be-fore he said the words . . . it came into my mind. He's going to tell ev-erybody's he's gay." This "pseudotherapeutic managed event" was live theater—"incredibly dramatic and very painful." Although Mark had a sense of what his father was going to say, it still did not take away from the initial shock: "it felt very surreal." Mark describes feeling outside himself, "where you're kind of looking at all this stuff through your eyes." However, shock quickly gave way to the "core response"—anger and a sense of betrayal about "being lied to for so long."

This seems intimately tied to the underlying feeling of frustration about not really ever completely knowing his father. Mark describes the fact that he "chased him a lot as a younger man and . . . as an adolescent trying to sort of get close to him." And although this piece of information was "very helpful" and "explained a lot of things," his father remains to some extent "very distant," a man "really hard to feel connected to."

The aftermath to the disclosure proved frustrating in certain ways too. John wanted to "manage" his family's reactions. He wanted his sons to participate in his own therapy and "work through this" with him. "I want to hear your feelings about this," John insisted. Mark countered by declining the invitation at first. He had a sense at the time that although his father did want to hear, he "also didn't want to hear." Eventually, Mark did go to a session with his dad which proved "liberating" in asserting his right to "go through this at [his] pace."

Although Mark admires his father for his bravery in exposing his homosexuality, which ultimately seemed to have moved their own relationship as well as the relationships with others in their family to a more intimate level, he thinks that his father is still unaware of how much and for how long "the hiding [and] the divulging . . . controlled family life." Both "the release . . . of the secret and the process of getting through it" were, according to Mark, "self-centered" acts. Although cognizant of the "huge stigma attached to . . . being gay," the issue for Mark is "much more about how [his father] dealt with that fact than who he chooses . . . to share his bed with." It was concealment of the secret rather than the secret itself that was most troubling. *Unveiling* the secret, however, proved crystallizing for Mark. Suddenly he was able to see, similar to reading an eye chart while looking through just the right "lens." Memories were now "framed with this new information." The pieces finally all fit together.

His dad being gay has made homosexuality a personal experience for Mark, difficult to dismiss, as many do, as just "immoral" or as just "right or wrong." For him, that's too simplistic. He has had to come to terms with his feelings about it in a way that others not as personally affected by it do not. Although the reflection of those feelings has been expanding, it has been uncomfortable as well. Consideration of his father as a sexual being and the dynamics of the actual physical attraction have been a source of discomfort to be sure, but he credits himself with trying to see more clearly those things that others "don't really want to" see. His natural capacity to think and reflect about himself and the world around him has been aided and expanded by the events he has had to confront and vice versa. The occurrence of those events has helped him to develop his capacity to think and reflect on a deeper level than he might have had those events never transpired. "Maybe just really big things have to happen to change your whole perspective," he concludes.

With new information comes new understanding. He is able to "look back" at what was and see it now in a different light, with new eyes, almost transforming the memory itself. His mother's intense rage at his father and his father's need to hide have both assumed a new context. The sense of enlightenment that results from new understanding has the possibility, he says, to "really change how you feel about things that have happened to you. That's . . . very heartening. . . . I have a deep trust in that."

ANDY

I wish he was here. I wish he was still alive.

Jeanette and Miguel, Andy's parents, were both born in Cuba, where they met and fell in love. When Castro came to power, Jeanette managed to get out of the country before Miguel, going to Spain in the meantime. Although she initiated the necessary paperwork to get him out, five years went by before they saw each other again. When they finally did, sparks flew, resulting in a hasty marriage. Andy was conceived in Spain, in the honeymoon suite, about twenty-seven years ago. A few months later the couple immigrated to the United States.

Their marriage turned out to be a mistake, a temporary solution to the obvious fact that they had grown apart after their five-year separation. The stress of coming to a new country and neither knowing the language nor the customs—"culture shock"—the stress of the pregnancy, Miguel's stress about not feeling "prepared" for family life, all contributed to their decision to divorce shortly after Andy was born. Miguel left, temporarily moved to New York City, then permanently moved to Florida. Andy and his mother lived by themselves for the next nine years.

From the age of seven, Andy regularly saw his father, mostly during Christmas and summer vacations. He vividly recalls the times they shared—Disney World, Sea World, the beach. Miguel owned a 1982 red Mustang convertible, had a beautiful house surrounded by gardens, a waterfall, and about 100 finches. Andy remembers helping his father protect the birds by putting guards up around their nests so that "garter snakes wouldn't eat the eggs." Two lovebirds completed the idyllic scene. Caesar, the parrot, resided inside the house: "I hated Caesar. I couldn't feed him without him trying to bite my finger off." Andy fared better with the dog Rex, a boxer. Rex used to keep Andy company when Miguel was busy at work in his hair salon. Socially adept, seductive, charismatic, a talented guitarist and singer, and extremely good looking, Miguel had it all. "He was really cool," says Andy, apparently a consensus held by everyone, including Vito, Miguel's "steady roommate" for many years, a man who worked as a flight attendant and with whom Andy shared many fun-filled hours.

In stark contrast was Neil, Andy's stepfather, who came into the picture when he was ten years old. A truck driver by trade, he and Andy "never really got along." The competition between them was fierce, each feeling the need to protect himself, each feeling the need for control. Although Neil proved "a knight in shining armor" for Jeanette—enabling her and her son to finally get out of the projects and move into a three-family house in the suburbs—for Andy, Neil was "a hard worker" but an "ignorant" man who understood and cared little about him. When Andy would make halfhearted attempts to assist his stepfather with "doing stuff around the house," Neil would frequently make comments such as, "Oh shut up, little one," or "Leave me alone. I know what I'm doing," even suggesting to Jeanette that Andy "pay rent" when he started to work part-time at age sixteen. "He never tried to be my friend" is how Andy sums it up. Although Jeanette tried to remain oblivious to what was going on between the two of them, she would usually side with her husband, something that Andy remains hurt and angry about.

Prior to Andy's own marriage several months ago, his mother tried to convince him to invite Neil's family to the wedding, all ten brothers and sisters, even though it had been many years since Andy had seen any of them. Never feeling respected or especially liked by them, Andy opted out of family get-togethers in the past, avoiding contact whenever possible. Jeanette's plea that he invite them because, after all, "How's that gonna look?" triggered the first mother-son confrontation ever in which Andy clearly and finally told his mother that he "blamed" her for "always favoring" Neil: "You always wanted to do what he did and what I wanted to do . . . didn't matter."

With all the conflict at home, going to Florida to visit his father was a relief, although when Andy was about fifteen, things began to change there too. Miguel struggled for years to save money in order to bring his *own* family—father, mother, and sister—from Cuba to the United States. He finally succeeded. After they settled here, Andy felt pressured by his father to spend time with them. Especially irksome was his sometimes paranoid and always "nagging" grandmother. Vacations did not seem "as much fun" anymore and he began to spend less time in Florida, preferring to stay at home with his friends or go to Spain to visit relatives.

When Andy was seventeen, Miguel became very ill with liver cancer, or so Andy was told at the time. His illness had progressed dramatically when Andy visited that summer. The following February, Andy received a call that his father would probably not "make it through the night." By the time he got on a plane and got down there, Miguel had passed away. It was Valentine's Day.

The funeral was heightened by the presence of Vito, Miguel's "best friend." It was only after *he* came in that Andy began to feel more connected to what was happening and more connected to the depth of his loss: "I get chills now because I remember seeing him at the door. . . . He hugged me, I hugged him, and we both cried together." Andy felt that Miguel's mother and sister were just crying because "their relative died. But me and Vito, I felt like we were crying 'cause we loved him." Several months later, it was Andy's aunt, his mother's sister, who told him the truth: his father had died of AIDS. He was forty-eight.

Over time, Andy began to slowly and inevitably put the clues about his father's sexuality together. The whole family seemed to be observing a pact of silence. But since he was not asking, they were not telling. He wonders:

> Did my dad not want to tell me and, if so, why? Did my mom not want me to find out and asked him not to tell me? Were they ashamed? Did they think I would turn gay?

A few months before his own wedding, Andy sat down with Isabel, his girlfriend of seven years, telling her of his suspicions that his father might have been gay. As if to prepare her, warn her, perhaps, of the inevitable, he asked her how she might feel if that turned out to be true. "Would that bother you?" he wanted to know. Without flinching, she replied, "Your dad *was* gay." Ten minutes of silence followed. His surprise gave way to relief: "Wow. . . . You know what? I love him anyway." The unknown had finally become known—"no more guess-work." Isabel told him that her own mother, a good friend of Andy's maternal aunt, informed her of that fact right after she started to date Andy. Her mother said to her, "I know his aunt. And his dad was gay," to which Isabel swiftly replied, "I don't care." Andy was reassured by Isabel's interest in him and felt lucky to have found someone so accepting and so committed to their relationship so early on. Subsequently, Andy informed his aunt that he had spoken with Isabel and now knew the truth about his father, emphasizing to her that his feelings about him, the love that he always felt for him, had not and would not change.

As to the secrecy surrounding his father's homosexuality and his death from AIDS, Andy thinks that no one was talking with him about it out of their need to protect him, worrying "about how [he] would react to" the disclosure, pointing to the prejudice against homosexuals that pervades Cuban culture. If one is perceived as feminine in any way, one is quickly labeled a *maricon* [a fairy].

Not only has he never spoken with his mother about it—their recent confrontation about inviting Neil's family to the wedding being "enough" discussion for now—he has never spoken with any of his friends about it either, fearing they would "not feel as comfortable" with him. Since his dad was gay, would they begin to wonder, "Hey, maybe he's a little gay" himself? Although "one hundred percent heterosexual," he is concerned about how his friends might react. Perhaps years from now, after these relationships have long been established, he may say to them, "Hey, read this book and figure it out." Then again, perhaps he will never disclose: "I'd like to feel someday that I can trust my friends enough to know that part of me and that they would still love me the same. . . . But I don't know that." Sometime in the not-too-distant future he may consider asking his aunt the full story. For right now, he knows as much as he wants to.

Over time, Andy has become more aware of another layer of feeling—anger about the secrecy surrounding his father's homosexuality. Admittedly, it is difficult for him to be angry with his father, now gone, and difficult to be angry with his mother, who spent much of her life struggling. Yet he is.

> I feel that they have deprived me and themselves of a lot of important things in life, things that I am learning now as an adult and it is much harder. I don't care that my dad was gay. I care that nobody told me.

Although Miguel has been absent from his son's life for about ten years now, he has never been absent from his son's thoughts. He considers their similarities and differences. His mother and aunt remind him how much he takes after his father at times—the way he looks, the way he gestures—"which is kind of funny to me . . . since I didn't grow up next to him," Andy says, amused. He is more aware of their differences. Miguel was more "the leader of the pack," always the one to organize and direct. Andy considers himself more of a follower, a leader only by default: "I'm not the one in charge unless everybody else gets out of hand," although he does acknowledge being "the safety guy, the responsible one," the conscience of the group when necessary.

Miguel's influence on his son's character has been critical. In a psychology course Andy took in college, all the students were asked to complete a test designed to measure their degree of androgyny. Andy's score fell right "in the middle." Choosing a profession such as social work, one which emphasizes caring for others, attests to his comfort with his feminine side, while simultaneously being able to "take charge" when the situation calls for it, attests to his comfort with his masculine side. "I like the way I am," Andy emphatically states.

Andy mourns the loss of his father. He is sad that Miguel could not have been more a part of his life when he was younger, sad that he is not a part of it now, sad that he will never be again: "I wish he was here. I wish he was still alive." Andy feels that he would be immeasurably enriched if he were. More conservative, less worldly than his father, Miguel exposed his son to a slice of life he never would have seen in the predominately Cuban community of his small New Jersey town. Andy hopes to locate Vito someday. Only through him could he really find out about those parts of his father that still remain a mystery.

In some ways, Andy feels that he has had to develop on his own, trying to figure out all by himself or with God's help "what a guy does." He would have liked to share his confusion and indecision more directly with his father. Gay or not gay, he would have liked the opportunity to ask him, "Hey, Dad . . . this is the situation I'm in. Any advice? What did you go through?" He acknowledges talking to his father "all the time" though—in church or before drifting off to sleep. Andy asks his father to "give [him] a hand" during the hard times and knows Miguel is "looking out for [him]" during the good times: "I feel like I wouldn't be where I am now if he wasn't backing me up."

Although no one could take the place of the father he longs for, he has the companionship of his wife, one who accepts and loves him for *all* that he is. Andy says that he will be forever grateful to her for trying to keep the memory of his father alive by "remembering to put a flower in church every Valentine's Day, . . . light[ing] a candle every birthday of his, and for still loving me."

NOAH

My life has been more a model of how . . . things can go right.

Noah considers himself a pretty lucky guy. Now a medical student, he was born twenty-three years ago in a large Canadian town. His parents—Cheryl, age forty-eight, and Dennis, age fifty—met at a modeling agency that employed them both—his mother as a receptionist, his father as a model. They were married for six years before deciding to separate and divorce. As Noah understands it, Cheryl left Dennis because of his tendency to be hurtful. For example, Dennis would call attention to Cheryl's weight problems by storing ice cream in the freezer and then berating "her for having no willpower when she ate it." His mother met her second husband, Bart, before she and Dennis separated; his father met *his* "husband," Ron, about four years later. Both couples remain happily together to this day. Cheryl and Dennis remain good friends.

Both parents reportedly "worked double time" prior to their son's birth so that they could both be with him full-time for the first eighteen months of his life. Noah's early memories of family life revolve mostly around time spent with his father. Dennis and Cheryl tried their hand at acting—their reason for coming from Canada to New York City in the first place—which meant that they had to get "real jobs waiting tables." Since Dennis was "less tolerant of being treated badly," he was out of work more often than Cheryl was. So he would spend much of his free time at home playing with his son. Noah's first memory of his father is of them finding a blackboard in the garbage one day, bringing it home, washing it, resurfacing it, and then sitting together in front of it, discovering the world of words together.

The summer before his parents separated, Noah, then age five, was sent to Canada for twelve weeks, where he stayed in the homes of various relatives—grandparents on both sides, aunts, and uncles. The time he spent away from his parents was difficult. He recollects: "Every night, I ended up calling them and crying on the phone 'cause I missed them. . . . It's like a first time I was going away to camp, but it wasn't camp." When he returned home, his mother discussed the possibility of his going to San Francisco to live with her and Bart. His father was to remain in New York. Bart was a university professor who was planning on taking a sabbatical there. More recently, Noah spoke with his mother about their decision to go to San Francisco at that time. He says that she recalls he was reluctant but superficially agreed to it. In retrospect, he is not clear he really understood the decision they were making.

That event was "traumatic" for Noah. The separation from his father was extremely difficult: "I remember the first month we were in [San Francisco], I pretty much talked to him on the phone every day and ended up . . . crying at night 'cause he wasn't there." After the academic year was over, they moved back to New York City, getting an apartment about a mile from his father: "I saw both my parents all the time . . . it was pretty great." Noah was six.

During the next decade, Noah would frequently "yo-yo back and forth between [his] mom and [his] dad . . . whatever was more convenient." He seemed to enjoy the freedom and the stimulation that came with living in two separate households simultaneously. The "after-school specials and . . . bad TV movies" that depicted children living lives fraught with conflicted alliances—"Oh, no. I'm at one house or the other"—was not a situation he could relate to at all. His situation "was pretty chill . . . always was."

One Saturday afternoon when Noah was about nine years old, he asked his father whether they could go see the movie *Robocop*. Not sure of what he was getting himself into, father agreed anyway, bringing his date, Ron, along for Noah to meet. The unrelenting violence of the first fifteen minutes was all Ron could take. He left the theater. Dennis insisted on leaving with Noah too. For the rest of the afternoon, Noah acted like "an obnoxious little shit," making sure that everyone felt just as miserable as he did. His chant: "But you said we could see the movie. We should see the movie. You said we could see the movie" was repeated ad nauseum until Ron, usually a man of infinite patience, had had enough and left the scene. "Everyone felt bad," Noah recalls with clarity. Future meetings went better, however. Since Ron owned a VCR and his father didn't, Noah would stay at Ron's house watching movies when the two men went out.

Always "a fairly aware kid," Noah seemed to have been conscious of his father's homosexuality all along. Assorted male friends Dennis had at the time, including an actor and an opera singer, Noah thinks, were all gay: "By the time I was in third grade, I could generally tell when someone was or wasn't." Also being a very imaginative kid, that awareness was confirmed one day while "rootin' through [his] dad's closet just for stuff to play with." His father always had an array of costumes—"shawls and capes and belts"—which Noah freely made use of. The closet also contained an array of "dirty magazines . . . of a homosexual nature" which "pretty much sealed the deal." Not wanting to embarrass his father, Noah "didn't say anything to him"; rather, he "just put them back."

One afternoon a few months later, Dennis took his son aside and said, "[Noah], I have something to tell you." Being pretty sure what his father was going to reveal, Dennis couldn't quite get it out: "Well, what do you want me to say?" Sensing that his father needed some encouragement, Noah offered, "Well, why don't you just tell me the truth?" Father replied, "Well, I mean, do you want me to say that [Ron] and I are lovers?" "Is that the truth?" Noah wanted to know.

Dennis finally said, "Yes," asking his son if he was okay with that. Noah told him that he was and that he had "figured it out a while ago." He thinks that his father felt "relieved." For Noah, "it wasn't an issue."

He claims that "it wasn't an issue" for most of his friends at that age either. When one of them used the word *fag,* he promptly spoke up, "Don't use that word." When his friend wanted to know why, Noah asked him if he knew his dad and liked his dad. When the answer came back yes on both counts, Noah explained, "My dad's gay. . . . So you shouldn't use that word 'cause it's not nice." Noah says that revealing this to his close friends was not that much of a risk since their group was "really tight." Five of them traveled in a pack, going everywhere together: "I sort of knew that I could trust them and that they were cool." Growing up in a liberal New York environment "always surrounded by a lot of diversity of all sorts" helped. Having "yo-yoed around" to different schools much of his life, thus being exposed to a wide range of experiences, was also a factor in his being nonchalant about it all. Cheryl, too, was apparently always accepting of her ex-husband's homosexuality. In fact, when she and Bart purchased a summerhouse, it was common for Dennis, Ron, and Noah to go there with them to spend the weekend.

Although Dennis's homosexuality was not an issue for Noah or for Cheryl, it *was* an issue for Dennis's mother. Raised a devout Catholic and having lived on a farm for much of her life, she was not prepared to accept the reality of a gay son, cutting off communication with him for a while and refusing to call the house after Ron moved in. "There was some strife there," is how Noah puts it. More recently Dennis, Ron, and Noah have gone to visit his grandmother in Canada on two occasions "and now everything is hunky-dory," although Noah is unsure "exactly how that got resolved."

When Noah was fifteen years old, his mother, Bart, and he moved permanently to the West Coast where they have lived for the past eight years. Usually, Noah flies in to see his dad. However, on one occasion, Dennis went there under the guise of attending "some conference-type thing." Noah thought that a bit odd since his father was not working at the time. One day during his visit he announced to Noah that he had a tape he wanted him to watch. Once it started, Dennis asked his son, "Do you recognize that person?" Without missing a beat, Noah said, "Yeah, it's you in a swimsuit with a wig on." "What do you think?" Dennis was anxious to know. "I think you're good at it," Noah said with amusement. Apparently, the so-called "conference" turned out to be a "pageant" for drag performers. Dennis was now surer of himself—and more glamorously adorned—for *this* disclosure, a kind of second coming out for him.

Although his father has a more traditional job in the antiques business, he spends the majority of his time creating cabaret material along with "fantastical costumes," performing in different venues all over the city. Noah comes to town every time his father puts together a new show. When not otherwise occupied, they will "hang out" and just enjoy each other's company—now more of a "peer relationship" than anything else, Noah thinks. Active in the drag community, Dennis was recently doubly crowned "runner-up Miss New York" *and* Miss Fire Island. Noah keeps pictures on his wall of his father, the reigning queen, dressed in full regalia. When people ask, "Is that your mom?" he pipes back, "Actually, that's my dad!"

For Noah, his father's homosexuality has historically meant greater exposure to a wider range of ideas. In seventh grade, for example, that translated into having "some interesting fashion choices." While everyone else in his class dressed in jeans and tee shirts—Gap style—Noah was looking through the latest *International Male* catalog, which his father always had laying around, for suggestions on what to wear. One time he ordered a pair of multicolored, oversized, "billowy" beach pants, which "looked very good on the model." However, wearing them to school resulted in "the most horrific experience of [his] life." Kids hurled taunts such as, "Nice clown pants" or "You look like a stained-glass window," making it "possibly the longest day ever." Similar to his father, Noah concedes that he can be "flamboyant" at times.

Besides that particular trait, Noah acknowledges that he and his dad are similar in other ways too. Both like to feel that they are just "fundamentally better at doing things" and are more knowledgeable than others. Noah finds himself "correcting people" as his dad does, although he will admit this quality always "horrified" him. His mother took him out of a certain private school he attended for one year because he had challenged the teacher's authority by openly correcting her grammar.

To be sure, there are differences between them. Their worldviews sometime collide. Noah considers himself "more tolerant" than his father. Having been brought up religiously mixed—Jewish and Catholic—in a "very open-minded" way, "aware of everything" is in stark contrast to his dad, who attended Catholic school during most of his childhood and who "grew up on a farm milking cows." Noah has occasionally confronted him about his subtle bigotry, pointing out that he "judges entire groups of people . . . based on certain nationalist cab drivers." But Dennis defends himself, acknowledging that his opinions are grounded in experience "observed over years and years."

Noah is clear that his thoughts and feelings about his father have nothing at all to do with his homosexuality per se. Rather, they are based on other character traits. For example, Noah experiences his "puritanical" stance as hypocritical. Although Dennis claims to be against pornography, at least at one point in his life he had a collection large enough and obvious enough for his son to have stumbled onto. Noah also has difficulties reconciling his father—and his mother and their respective partners for that matter—as sexual beings. He felt extremely uncomfortable one time in high school when he thought he "almost walked in on" his father and Ron but considers that reaction a "fairly normal" one as most people do not "like the idea of their parents having sex"—gay or otherwise.

Noah feels that his father's homosexuality "was a good thing" for him. If someone has difficulties with it, "that was *their* problem . . . their short-sightedness." He has known other families in a similar predicament, either through his father's social network or through school and at times has been surprised at the difficulties this has posed for them. He says, "My family was just so wonderfully reasonable about the world that it sort of never occurred to me that other people weren't."

Noah admits that his approach to his dad's being gay has changed a bit over the years. Before he was inclined to tell his friends only when he decided it was "relevant." Those were occasions when someone would be spending the night or would use a derogatory term to describe a gay person. Now it comes up more naturally when others inquire about his family. It is also a way to "test the waters" and weed people out of his life early on if necessary.

Although Noah admits he was unhappy at the time his parents separated and divorced and found it difficult relocating as often as he did, he never doubted their love for him, genuinely feeling that he "was always first" in their lives, a situation he knows some other kids have not experienced. "I think I understand how lucky I was and, if any-thing, my life has been more a model of how . . . things can go right." The love he has felt coming from all four parents makes him feel for-tified enough to buffer any of life's problems: "And if three of them happen to be male and one of them happens to be female, then . . . that's cool."

Lucky, indeed.

JOSEPH

He really does love me very much. And I love my dad.

Joseph's parents, Ian and Jean, both age sixty-nine, had more in common than just their age. "High school sweethearts," they were both budding landscape painters who decided to go to Europe to-gether to further develop their craft. They stayed for four years before returning to the States as husband and wife. They brought their two children, Emily, then three years old, now forty-four, and Joseph, then one year old, now forty-two, back with them. Although Ian and Jean both exhibited their artwork in the 1960s and 1970s, over time Ian "put down the paints and the brushes" in favor of a career teach-ing art. Apparently that suited him better, a situation that guaranteed him stability—a paycheck every week, tenure, and a retirement plan.

Despite being "middle class," despite having to live in a tenement in a poorer section of the city and attending the public schools,despite brother and sister having to share a bedroom and a bunk bed, Joseph always felt taken care of during those early years of his life. Although he did not have the "privileges that wealthy children had" and felt en-vious at times of his "Park Avenue . . . friends" with their "enormous apartments . . . there was plenty of food on the table." Attention from his father was plentiful too. When a group of Joseph's friends decided to make go-carts for fun, he recalls his father scavenging for the parts—"tires and axles and wood"—so that, eventually, he had some-thing to be proud of: "I think I had one of the fastest ones."

Joseph recalls being "much adored as a kid." But that changed as he grew into adolescence. The mounting tension between Ian and Jean affected the relationship between Ian and Joseph. "Punish-ments" were commonplace as outlets for Ian's anger and frustration about feeling "stuck" in life. Finally, after twenty-two years, Ian left the home. Jean "was devastated"; Joseph was relieved, then "enraged." He was fifteen at the time.

He was also quite confused. He never spoke to his mother about what had happened or why it happened but was a "witness" to her "grief." Joseph mourned in his own way. He eventually joined a gang. All the pent-up anger and frustration of his own took an antisocial form. He was not only trying to deal with the dissolution of his family as he knew it, he was also trying to deal with his own conflicted sexual identity. Like husband and wife, father and son have much in common too. Both Ian and Joseph are gay.

At first a victim of the gang, a target for its collective rage, Joseph decided "to use [his] decorating skills," to help them design their emblem. He decided that since he couldn't "lick 'em, [he'd] join 'em." After that, he was accepted. A year or two later, the gang turned on him again. This time it was more serious. They attempted to sexually assault him. That was when he knew he had to get out. The ways he was dealing with all the internal and external turmoil he was experiencing were not working any longer. Another outlet—disco—was his salvation: "it . . . saved my life 'cause I had another platform . . . to go to." Clubbing became his new obsession.

Contact with his father continued unabated. After Ian left the family home, he was taken in by a woman "who had quite a bit of money." This arrangement lasted a few years. Joseph lived for a few months at a time with them and a few months with his mother: "I felt very torn. I didn't know where to go," he said. Despite his anger with his father, he still wanted and needed him. Joseph's sister Emily found another solution. At seventeen, she moved to the opposite coast to live, eventually establishing her own family, returning only infrequently: "She really escaped the madness."

Besides being gay, father and son have other similarities. Their physical "resemblance" is striking and "both are sensitive . . . types," interested in cooking, music, and, most of all, art. Their mutual passion for the latter also reveals their differences. Although Ian never pursued his craft beyond a certain point, preferring to take the safer academic route, Joseph struggled long and hard to establish himself as an artist specializing in a type of interior painting known as faux finish, now working for some of "the richest people in the world." Humorously he observes, "I finally got to be in those apartments that I dreamed about when I was little." Joseph sees his father as a more "complacent type"; he sees himself as "a dreamer." Their approach to dealing with their homosexuality demonstrates their differences too.

Joseph thinks that his father may not have had a real awareness of his own homosexuality until perhaps he was in his late forties, although he could have been interested in and possibly involved with men earlier. "I think that part of his life was quiet," Joseph reflects. Back in the 1960s and 1970s, Ian had been active in the artistic community in which drugs were prevalent and sexuality fluid and "ambiguous." So the day that Joseph, then around twenty years old, went over to his father's apartment for a party accompanied by his own boyfriend and found his father with *his* new boyfriend, although a surprise, was not really a shock. It took some adjusting to. Being gay himself made it a bit "easier."

On the contrary, Joseph was anything *but* quiet about his sexuality. In fact, at around the age of seventeen, both parents suggested to him that he was gay. Not being sure himself, he took offense. In retrospect, however, with all the "swishin' around . . . the floral print jackets and the . . . platform shoes . . . I think that it was pretty clear."

There are other differences as well. Joseph describes his father as "a relationship type." In fact, Ian is still with the same man that Joseph saw him with that day at the party over twenty years ago. The sort of relationship Ian has with his partner James, who is fifty-two years old, is one not only marked by a seventeen-year difference in their ages but also one with a distinct father-son quality about it. In fact, so "fatherly" does Ian feel toward James that he will sometimes "slip" and call son Joseph by his partner's name. In contrast, Joseph has not been in a long-term relationship for about ten years, preferring to focus on establishing himself professionally and do whatever work he had to do on himself first. "I guess I could be ready now," he considers. The kind of relationship he might want would also probably be more equal, more "yoke to yoke," than the one that he perceives Ian and James have.

To this day, Joseph has never spoken to his father about his separation from the family and the "complicated, multilayered" reasons that may have contributed to its occurrence, but it seems likely that his homosexuality was one of those reasons. Joseph speculates that had he been in a similar situation himself, with "something else calling," his solution would have been the same, despite the "hurt" that he might cause others along the way: "He had to do it so he could find happiness." This realization has moved the healing process along and helped to further solidify their relationship.

Joseph looks at his dad now and sees a man content with life. He salutes his courage "to face the music" and make the necessary changes to find what he truly needed—"his calling." Ian's capacity to find a relationship serves as a model for Joseph and holds out the hope that perhaps he, too, might achieve that one day.

Although having a gay father is not something he routinely shares with many, particularly not those he works with, he is boastful about it with his gay friends. Despite the trauma of his parents' separation, Joseph feels that his father always "shows up for" him, always tries to be genuinely mindful of what is happening in his life—truly the mark of "a good parent." Perhaps the most important commonality of all is the strong feelings shared by father and son: "He really does love me very much. And I love my dad."

RICHARD

I'm there for him.

In some ways, Richard is an average thirteen-year-old. He likes to build models, ride his bicycle, fix his remote control car, play with his computer, spend time with his friends, and "have as much fun as possible." I met with him while he was on a class trip to Washington, DC, designed to expose him and his classmates to the workings of our government. Richard has lived most of his life in Nome, Alaska, except for a brief time as an infant when he and his mother spent a few months in California preparing his grandmother to uproot and come north with them.

In some other ways, Richard is special. An only child, he alternates living two weeks at a time with his mother, Katherine, a secretary, and two weeks with his father, Charles, a manager of an office supply company. Both are forty-two years old. Richard likes this arrangement because his parents live right next door to each other in the same housing complex, so he gets to see both of them virtually all the time. Katherine and Charles divorced in 1997 after a fifteen-year marriage. Richard doesn't know why that was: "They don't want to tell me yet." He remembers the time right before his parents' divorce as being "pretty scary," the time when they were "continuously arguing and fighting and just . . . being mad." One thing *is* clear, though: his father is gay. Whether that contributed to his parents' split, he doesn't know.

Richard's early memories of his father are vague. He recalls some good times together—going fishing and hunting, trips to his grandmother's, and the famous rubber ducky race. Apparently a favorite in his part of the country, this involves the purchase of a rubber ducky, which gets a unique number. All the rubber duckies are then dumped into the river, and the owner of the one that reaches the finish line first gets a prize. One year his father split $10,000 with several other people after their rubber ducky won. Although only three years old at the time, Richard recalls the excitement surrounding that event.

Richard describes his dad as "easygoing" and community minded. If someone needs help, they can always count on Charles. About father-son similarities, Richard points out a physical likeness with his father, except for the fact that his dad has a beard and he does not: both are big and tall, both are chubby faced, and both have curly hair.

As for their differences, Richard talks "a lot more" than his dad does. He is usually the one to initiate a conversation. His father does not converse unless he has to. Richard wishes the situation were different. He would like to know more about what his father's "exact feelings" and his "views" about him are and the ways he thinks he should conduct himself. Overall, Richard rates their relationship as "pretty close": "He's my father."

One conversation Charles *did* start about three years ago was telling Richard he is gay. Although he doesn't recall his father's exact words, Richard *does* recall being "a little surprised" by the news, even a bit shocked, also "a little scared," not knowing how his friends might react. His recollection about that conversation was his dad telling him that, having come out as a gay man, he was now "really happy" but worried that the news might sadden his son. Reportedly, Charles was quite surprised at how well Richard took the disclosure and relieved that he seemed "okay with it."

Thus far, no one else in their family knows, except for Richard's mom, who found out accidentally through her female co-worker. Charles had attended an event known as the Banishment Ball, a celebration for Mr. and Miss Gay Alaska. The co-worker, also in attendance, saw Charles and then informed Katherine of her ex-husband's presence. Richard spoke with his mother afterward and thinks she had already suspected Charles was gay, although he had never informed her directly.

As of yet, Richard has not told anyone about his father's sexuality. He thinks that since Charles has not disclosed to his family or friends, he shouldn't tell anyone either: "Until he's okay with it, I shouldn't be okay with it." If Richard does eventually decide to tell his friends, he hopes it will not make any difference to them. Since most have relatives who are gay, he thinks it wouldn't "be such a big deal." However, he cannot be sure and doesn't want to chance it right now.

Richard honestly admits to questioning his own sexuality after his father disclosed. Although he "like[s] girls," he thinks it is too early for him to say that he is definitely one way or the other: "So far, I haven't . . . made my decision."

In the three years since the disclosure, Richard has seen and been exposed to "new people" and "new perspectives." He regularly attends PFLAG meetings, Bear meetings, and other gay-related events. Sometimes Charles hosts the meetings. If Richard is home, he participates. If the meetings are somewhere else, sometimes he will go; other times he will not. It depends on how much homework he has. Attending a "strict Catholic school" with several hours of assignments a night doesn't leave time for much else.

About this interview, Richard says that he is doing it to support his dad and "for other kids who . . . need help" dealing with a situation he has had to face. Richard knows his father is happy that his son is "there for him."

What father wouldn't be?

SHAWN

Our relationship now is as good as it has ever been.

Shawn has moved around a bit during his thirty-one years. He spent the first six months of his life in Oklahoma City, the next five years in Wheaton, Illinois, then thirteen years in Fairfax, Virginia, before going off to college in California. For the past decade, Washington State has been his home. Those early moves were necessitated by his father David's work as a chemical engineer. Now sixty years old, David was employed by several major corporations and "was one of the preliminary brains that gave the world the plastic pop bottle." Shawn's mother, Pamela, now fifty-five, also an academic, is a high school Latin teacher. The two were introduced by mutual friends.

Shawn recalls "a lot of love in the household" of his childhood. Pamela stopped teaching when her son was born, stayed home until he reached school age, then resumed her career. Music filled the house: David on bagpipes, Shawn on piano, saxophone, drums, and guitar at different points along the way. Mom was an avid fan—Bill Withers, the Beatles, Gordon Lightfoot, and Jim Croce all had their special place. Shawn retains a memory of watching his father play in his Scottish bagpipe band around the time he was three or four years old. Those were good times.

Shawn's musical side always received a great deal of support from both parents while he was growing up as well as now from his fiancée, Linda, a musician herself. Although he currently works as an office manager by day, he plays in one of his four bands by night. For Shawn, music is not only a "necessary ingredient of life," it is a means of "survival": "the time on this earth when I'm closest to God." He also has his own record label and publishing company. Spirituality assumes a major role in his life, too. Born an Episcopalian, he just finished a three-year term on the vestry of his local parish. Making music and being in church are times when he feels he is at his best, making all the lesser moments in life seem worthwhile, happiest when he feels like "an active participant in the act of creation."

Despite the support from his father at times, Shawn never felt especially close to him while growing up. Although his dad read to him, taught him how to ride a bike, taught him about music—"the ins and outs of a hi-fi," how to compile audiotapes, even bought him a set of toy bagpipes—a sense of intimacy was missing. "Always the disciplinarian," David wanted his son to achieve, demanding only his "best" at all times, demanding "excellence." Their differing ideas about what his "best" was didn't seem to matter to his father. This was the way David was raised by his parents, and this was the way he was going to raise his son. Perhaps there were more complicated reasons that David adopted this particular style of parenting—reasons Shawn couldn't possibly have comprehended at the time.

When he was ten years old, his parents separated. They had been together for eleven years. His mother and father, his family, his "refuge and safety," everything that he had known and loved "was

blowing up for reasons [he] didn't understand." Although he had observed tensions between them, they told him that there did not seem
to be any real way to work out their mutual differences:

> I was an only child and it seemed there was nowhere to turn to. I
> wanted my family to remain intact, whole. That was the difficult
> part—the knowledge that this was beyond my control. . . . I was
> pissed off at both of them for becoming exactly what I didn't
> want them to become—divorced; I was hurt because I thought
> that it was my fault—a notion they quickly dispelled; [I was]
> confused because I didn't know what was going to happen after
> all of this. I clutched to [my] teddy bear for comfort and cried
> my eyes out.

Prior to the divorce, the family took a trip to San Francisco, visiting David's friends who played the organ at the local church. There,
in the Castro district, Shawn "saw two men holding hands." Curious,
he asked his parents about it. They responded "that some people were
that way." After the divorce, Pamela started to date, but his father
didn't. Shawn wondered why. His dad's move out of their home to
near Dupont Circle, an area heavily populated by gay men in Washington, DC, heightened his confusion, as did David's more permanent relocation to San Francisco in 1981. Whatever concerns he
had—conscious or subliminal—mostly centered on himself and his
already compromised standing with his peers due to being overweight. If his father were gay, would that new piece of information be
another source of ridicule for him?

On a visit with his father that summer, as they rode along Interstate
101 returning from a visit to David's parents' home, he informed his
son, "You're at an age where you know that San Francisco has a large
population of gay men. Well, I'm one of them." Shawn doesn't recall
any surprise, any agitation, or anything really negative on his part. He
was mostly relieved. His immediate response was: "So, what's for
dinner?" It was a confirmation of what he had briefly wondered about
for a while. "There is a certain peace that comes from knowing the
truth," he says with conviction. Despite all the anxiety his father
seemed to bring to the disclosure, Shawn considered it "a nonevent."
He was twelve at the time.

Learning about his father's homosexuality early on turned out to
be a helpful thing. He was old enough to fully comprehend what it

meant to have a gay father and young enough to not have yet internalized negative societal stereotypes. It was also around this time that he saw the video *Not All Parents Are Straight:*

> Seeing that tape sort of cemented the fact that I didn't have to be ashamed of him, I didn't have to be afraid of him, and I certainly didn't have to be . . . concerned with what other people thought about him. It was confirmation that I wasn't the only one who had grown up with this set of circumstances.

Finally he felt he wasn't alone.

As the reality began to sink in, he started to ask his father a bit more about being gay, wanting to know when and where those feelings originated. To be sure, there was some anger at him as well. Although he didn't quite understand it all then, he was aghast that his father had the audacity to sue his mother. Location apparently was key, he was to find out later. Had she sued him in a conservative Virginia court, he would have been "fried" and full custody would have, undoubtedly, gone to her. But since they agreed on joint custody, a suit in a more liberal District of Columbia court served them both well.

Shawn and his mother dialogued all along the way. Pamela knew about her husband's homosexuality only right before their separation and felt deeply resentful at the time. She had made a lifelong commitment to their relationship and was not prepared for this. Religiously raised in a small Midwestern town, it was all "far outside anything resembling her frame of reference." Her fear that David would somehow "turn [their son] gay" was a concern at first, but since Shawn was so obviously attracted to girls those fears eventually dissipated.

Two years after the divorce, Pamela married John, a therapist and minister. He had three children from a previous marriage. Although Shawn "resented" John's takeover of *his* home and the ways in which he doled out discipline to him as opposed to his more "lax" style with his own children, Shawn was mostly angry with his mother, who was only too "eager" to reconstruct a sense of family. In the process, Shawn felt that his needs "got lost in the shuffle," and he became "difficult, insubordinate, [and] disrespectful." The marriage lasted only about three years. Shawn has not seen any of the members of his stepfamily since he was fifteen, although Pamela still sees John socially. Shawn and his mother have since been able to reestablish their own connection.

Longing to talk with others about his family situation, Shawn tried to discuss it with a few of his cousins, who made him even more anxious by raising the possibility of his father contracting HIV. He also attempted to bring it up with his grandparents, who wanted to avoid the issue altogether. Dissatisfied, he wanted to find other kids in a similar circumstance. Over time he was able to disclose to a few of his classmates who could be trusted, avoiding any discussion about it with those who couldn't be.

> I wanted so badly to find some other kids of gay parents when I was a teen, mostly because I wanted to find a place to belong. I wanted to meet people who knew what I knew, who felt what I . . . felt.

As Shawn got older, his relationship with his father deepened. They spent summers together and a few holidays during the year. Learning how to shave was an experience Shawn recalls fondly. Anxious at first, his father showed him that if he took proper "care," there was little cause for concern. He also exposed his son to the sights and the sounds of more liberal San Francisco, a far cry from his Virginia home. Shawn was learning how to be a man.

But David became increasingly concerned about how his homosexuality would be perceived by others in regard to his capacity to raise a child. He wanted his life to "be proof that you can be gay and still be an effective parent." So he dealt with those concerns by becoming even "more of a hard head" than before, even more "inflexible": "he was a bit of a drill sergeant." (Being a former captain in the Army didn't help.) Shawn's grades—nothing less than an A would do—and his appearance—"[h]e went ballistic when I . . . pierced my ears"—all came under intense scrutiny. Anything that would remotely suggest that his son might be gay—an "arty" or "effeminate" look—was strongly discouraged. David was worried about and sensitive to the fact that others, especially his family, might think he was encouraging his son along certain lines: "like father, like son."

But father *is* like son, in certain ways anyway. Although Shawn is, at his core, a man of music and spirituality, and his father is, at *his* core, a man of science, both have difficulties revealing their emotional sides, both are perfectionists, both have high expectations of themselves and others, both are strongly opinionated, both are "lone wolves"—more similarities than differences, to be sure. Shawn feels that he now understands those similarities and differences in a deeper way than just a few years before as a young adult, a time when he was grappling with feeling "disillusioned with the world," brought on, in part, by his mother's "near-fatal" car accident and his father's separation from his partner, Joseph. David met Joseph when Shawn was fourteen. The two were together for almost twelve years, a relationship "that changed [his father] for the better," a yin-yang sort of thing. Shawn is sad about this loss and worries that his dad is by himself now without "a circle of friends." However, work makes his father happy—traveling, teaching—and that tends to keep their relationship on an even keel.

Although Shawn says that even though his father being gay did not make that much of a difference in terms of their own relationship, it clearly made a difference in his own individual life. He now feels a greater tolerance for those unlike himself, experiences a greater willingness to stand up for the rights of those who are persecuted because of their differences, and has a greater appreciation for his family. What he did not like was the sense of isolation he felt, believing that he was the only kid who had a gay parent and the intense questioning he went through as an adolescent about his own sexuality. Although he realizes that many teenagers experience periods of sexual ambiguity, in his case the situation was made more complicated.

What has been satisfying for Shawn is watching his father claim his identity and "grow comfortable in his own skin." He understands the conflicts David must have suffered through all those years, loving his family and wanting to be part of them but also needing to be "true to himself ": "He did the best he could. Nobody taught him how to be a gay man." Shawn says with conviction, "Our relationship now is as good as it has ever been." That has to do with Shawn being an adult. His father being "comfortable in his own skin" helps too. What also helps is his firm belief in the fact both parents love him and are "there . . . no matter what."

But perhaps what is most effective in getting him through the challenges he faces is his ability to express himself through his music:

> All of the pain, the frustrations . . . get channeled into the expression . . . of that which is inside of you [and] is ultimately one of the most healing things. If I didn't have that outlet and if music wasn't such an important part of my spirituality, I don't think I would have dealt with anything all that well.

ROB

Life goes on.

Twenty-one-year-old Rob describes himself as "a rough-and-tumble kinda guy." He goes with the flow and doesn't "sweat the small stuff." His ability to adapt easily developed early on when he, his father Warren, now sixty, his mother Jane, now forty-six, and his brother Jerry, now eighteen, had to move from base to base while Warren served in the Air Force both here and abroad. Relocation became a fact of life. As a result, Rob now feels that he could deal with "pretty much anything thrown in front of" him. It is a skill that has come in handy.

His parents met while Warren was stationed in the South. Jane's father was also in the Air Force at the time. Jane's mother saw Warren at the officers' club and invited him to the house with the intention "of hitting on him." Warren wasn't interested in her but *was* interested in her daughter. He and Jane dated for a while and eventually married. She went to law school and, after Warren retired from the Air Force, so did he. Both now have a private law practice and reside outside Washington, DC.

Rob says that he and his father "have always had a great relationship," one that has remained that way over the years despite some ups and downs. A "stay-at-home dad" after his mom started law school, Rob feels that his father has been consistently responsive to his interests and needs. Whether it was showing him how to operate his Dukes of Hazzard Power Wheels scooter as a youngster, or teaching him how to play baseball when he was a bit older, or coming to his lacrosse games now that he's in college, or just sitting down and watching a football game together, Rob has always felt his dad's presence: "He's a great guy—definitely."

Describing him as organized ("He's got his sock drawer and his underwear drawer . . . all lined up by color"), with an offbeat sense of humor ("Stuff he finds funny nobody else really does"), and truthful to a fault ("I don't know why, but he . . . won't lie"), Rob can recall only one physical confrontation with his father. He was around age twelve and learning about water conservation in school. One morning they were in the bathroom together. Rob observed Warren doing the unthinkable: he left the water running while combing his hair. Thinking it needlessly wasteful, Rob turned the faucet off: "I need to conserve the water." His father turned it back on. Off and on, on and off, back and forth they struggled until his father warned, "If you don't stop being such a brat, I'm gonna smack you." "Go ahead!" Rob dared. Smack him he did. Rob doesn't see this as such a bad thing since he "kind of deserved it." Although challenges to authority clearly did go on, this confrontation proved more an "isolated" incident—the exception to the rule.

When Rob was thirteen, his parents called "a family meeting." "Something important" was about to happen. Ten-year-old Jerry panicked and began to cry. He thought he was finally going to learn the truth about himself—that he was adopted, a ridiculous idea considering how much he resembled his mother when she was around his age. Everyone had a good laugh about that; they rib him about it even to this day. No, this was not about Jerry. It was about Jane. She finally revealed to her sons that she was a lesbian. Although Rob recalls feeling shocked at the time, he had suspected it. About a year before, the entire family, including Warren, had moved yet again, this time into the home of Jane's "friend," although Rob was unaware that it was her home: "I just thought we were moving out of the city." The two women shared a bedroom, and the boys would overhear them being affectionate. His shock readily gave way to acceptance.

Three years later, when Rob was sixteen, his father, then fifty-four, called him and his brother together again, this time without their mother. Flatly, Warren came right out with it: "I'm a homosexual. Is that OK with you?" Rob told his father that it was and that he already had some suspicions. "Really?" Warren asked. "Yeah," his son replied. "All right," Warren said. End of discussion. The two boys went downstairs and resumed watching television.

Jane knew about her husband's homosexuality all along. Apparently there had been "rumors" on the naval base. Getting married and having kids had helped them both. It provided "a cover" for him and an escape for her. Jane's family is riddled with "psychoreligious fanatics" who are against anything they perceive as non-Christian, such as homosexuality. "If you're a homosexual, you're the devil," according to most of them.

Although Rob did suspect Warren's homosexuality earlier, those suspicions were later in coming than those he had held about his mother. Warren was far less obvious about it. However, during a game of hide-and-seek, Rob stumbled upon his father's briefcase while hiding in the closet. He opened it and found it filled with gay pornography. After asking himself what the odds would be of having *two* gay parents, he tried to dismiss it. However, just having found out about his mom, coupled with his father's obvious disinterest in dating women after the separation, led him to consider the possibility more seriously: "Well, it could be."

For Rob, his father's disclosure was made smoother by the precedent set by his mother. He just accepts it as just another one of those things that sets his "quirky" family apart from the norm. Although he sometimes wishes his parents would have told him at the same time, he now realizes that that might have been too overwhelming for a thirteen-year-old to handle. Certainly, humor is one way he's dealt with it all. Rob thinks that having a gay mother *and* a gay father would make "a really funny [Jerry] Springer episode."

Warren's being gay was never really that much of an issue for his son. There were other concerns, such as how his father was going about meeting men and who those men could be. Making contact online and then arranging dates with people he didn't know was a scary thing to imagine his dad doing. Fears that his father would contract HIV, fears that he would get "the livin' crap" kicked out of him, and fears that he would die at the hands of homophobes out to destroy gay people, such as "Matt Shepard at Laramie," were all uppermost in his mind.

Most troublesome was the fact that his dad was dating younger men—much younger—around Rob's age, guys that could be his peers: "they . . . wanted to be 'buddy-buddy' with me." Confused and angry about this, Rob sought some professional help to understand his reaction, much as his brother Jerry had previously done. Two years prior to this, after their father came out, Rob moved away to go to college. During that time, Jerry became more aware of his father's activities and increasingly upset about whom his father was seeing. When Rob transferred back to a school in the area, he too became more aware of and more worried about his father's "choices," that is, what he considered his dad's poor judgment and impulsivity in matters of dating and sexuality. Rob came to understand he had an irrational fear that his father was trying to "replace" him with these other men. When he realized that he could never be replaced nor could their special father-son connection be duplicated, those fears dissipated.

One might think that having a gay mother and a gay father would lead some to question their own sexuality. Not Rob: he has always felt secure in his heterosexuality. He reports having a girlfriend since kindergarten and was the first in his group of friends to have sex: "I didn't really know what the hell I was doing, but I was doing it." That was in eighth grade. Unlike most of the guys in his peer group, he feels comfortable enough acknowledging an attractive guy without feeling any desire at all to have sex with him.

Although Rob has now disclosed to all of those friends, he was worried beforehand whether it would affect his friendships. One day, while his friends were in the basement drinking, playing pool, and watching television, he decided to tell them about his mother. He disclosed about her first because "it's more acceptable for a woman to be a lesbian to a bunch of guys that it is for a guy to be gay." Their consensus: "Yeah, we kind of figured that." He told them about his father next. Now all of them know and have been accepting of both of them and of Rob, even one "die-hard Republican" who considers Jane and Warren "different" and unlike most gay people. Trying to educate him on that point, Rob argues that most gays and lesbians are "like [his] mom and [his] dad pretty much."

Two years ago, Warren finally moved out of the family house and into his own apartment. After twenty-three years, his divorce to Jane was final. He was now on his own. Rob realizes how important this has been for his father: "I understand that . . . he's got a life . . . who am I to stop him?" At the same time, he sometimes longs for the way things were: "I kind of wished that he had stayed the way he was just 'cause that's how I knew him." Although Rob acknowledges the loss of his father as a "heterosexual . . . role model," he *never* felt the loss of him as a role model in general. Warren has shown his son how to be a father and a man. In the end, he concludes that his dad's homosexuality doesn't make any real difference to him: "He's still the same dad. He still loves me the same." In the end, "life goes on."

Life goes on for Rob, too. Now in his third year of college, he knows that he wants to be a high school history teacher, hopefully making a difference in the lives of young people. Believing in the "idea of history repeating itself," he is anxious to find out what the future will hold for him, how his own history may repeat itself. Whether his own son turns out to be straight or gay, if he "wants to play football or do ballet," it wouldn't make any difference to Rob: "I'll still be there."

Just like his dad.

ERIC

There's always an effort to find . . . pieces of my father.

Eric's mother Georgette, who died about fifteen years ago from cancer, and his father Robert, now seventy years old, knew each other as children in Cleveland. Although they grew up on different sides of the fence, their friendship blossomed in high school, leading to marriage when they were both eighteen years old. She worked as a waitress; he served four years in the Navy during the Korean War. Their first child, Rose, was born while Robert was still in the service. Always having "rules" for *everything,* Georgette didn't think that having only one child would be a wise choice, and so she asked her husband for another. Eric's birth forty-four years ago turned into "a deal," part of a package of compromises his parents reached in trying to negotiate a way to stay married *after* she learned about Robert's homosexuality two years into their eight-year marriage.

She made other demands on her husband as well—see a psychiatrist, never bring lovers into their house, and "be home for Sunday dinner." His father "gave in," at least at first. After his time in the Navy ended, he became a music student at the local conservatory and needed his wife's financial support in order to complete his studies. They were also good friends who liked and respected each other. Yet this arrangement broke down. Eventually, Robert stopped showing up for Sunday dinner. She then began the process of separation, not permitting him to see their children for about eight months after that.

One clear memory for Eric at around age four or five was seeing his father for the first time after those many months. Apparently he and his sister expressed confusion about where their father had gone and why he was no longer a part of their lives. So Georgette had called Robert to come for a visit, initiating an informal every-other-week visitation arrangement. As Robert made his way up the stairs to their second-floor apartment, Eric's excitement about seeing his father was uncomfortably juxtaposed with a sense of alienation from "this person [who] was a bit of a stranger" to him.

Eric describes the early relationship between Robert and himself as "absolutely wonderful." The two of them, along with Rose and his father's lover Jack took camping trips together, went to the zoo, to the movies, to museums, even to the World's Fair. When Eric and Rose would stay over on the weekends, their father tried hard to accommodate them, routinely taking one of the mattresses from the bedroom, where Eric and Rose would sleep, and placing it in the living room, where Robert and Jack would sleep. Getting up in the middle of the night on one occasion, Eric recalls watching Robert and Jack lying there side by side. The notion of "two men living together" piqued his curiosity at the time. "That seemed different to me in some way," he recalls, contrasting the life his mother had had with his father. Although he dismissed thinking too much about it, the novelty of it "would come and go" from his consciousness.

Eric describes his father in different ways, at once "remote . . . very difficult to . . . get at emotionally" yet "very gentle [and] soft-spoken," a man comfortable with children—his own and those of others. After Georgette remarried, two years after her separation and divorce, Robert bought Eric and Rose each a violin and would come to their home weekly to give them both lessons: "We were . . . his first students." Although Robert had odd jobs after completing his musical studies, he maintained his connection to music as well as a connection with his children by way of the violin. Eventually he built a thriving practice in their neighborhood.

Although Robert told his son that he had musical potential, Eric had limited patience and would practice only "an hour before" the weekly lesson. The potential conflict between Robert's role as father and his role as teacher were minimized by his good-humored, gentle approach. "I don't remember him *ever* losing his patience with me over that," he says gratefully. Rose was more dedicated and more disciplined and developed into a good amateur musician. She maintains more of a connection with her father in that way than does her brother.

Allowing the children to regularly see their father was not easy for Georgette. She dealt with weekend visits—one of her many "rules"— by insisting that neither of them be alone with Robert. Eric *and* Rose had to be present at all times. Her harshness and her rigidity—"drill sergeant-like"—all contributed to a "quirky" parenting style that directly affected the ways in which her children related to their father: "She had suspicions that there was something *not* safe about this. And . . . it turns out that she was right." Not for the reasons she may have thought though.

Nothing went on sexually between the father and the children or between Jack and the children, but Jack had his share of problems. Had the mother been aware of what those problems were, it is doubtful she would have continued to allow visitation, Eric thinks. Those problems were obvious right from the beginning of Jack's relationship with Robert. The two met forty years ago and moved in together in less than a week. Within that week, the police came to the door of their apartment, warning Robert that Jack was someone who was "not very kosher." Apparently Jack "had this thing for straight men," always trying to pick them up, forever getting into legal messes, and sometimes placing himself in serious danger. Robert was constantly rescuing Jack, which sometimes meant doing some financial juggling in order "to keep him out of jail"; at other times it meant moving out of the neighborhood entirely. Eric vividly recalls an incident in which Jack was attacked and knifed—arm in a sling, wounds all over his body. As a young boy, he did not understand what was going on with Jack, who seemed, on one level, a fun-loving sort of guy. But as Eric grew older, the reality became clearer: "There was something overbearing and strange about him."

Georgette's second marriage to Herbert, a patron at the diner where she worked, proved as conflict-ridden as her first marriage to Robert, only in different ways. In contrast to Robert, Herbert "was a beer-gutted . . . guy with a tattoo" who made his living as a telephone repairman. "A big guy in a big car," Georgette was not going to make the same error twice. Herbert was unmistakably straight, the ideal man for her children, so she thought. He turned out to be a gambler and a rageful alcoholic.

One evening after dinner, Herbert "made . . . a snide comment" about Robert. Eric, who was thirteen years old at the time, thinks it might have been precipitated by Herbert's frustration about Georgette's incessant idealization of Robert. Apparently, she would routinely go on about how intelligent, how well traveled, and what a good teacher Robert was. Robert was everything Herbert was not. It became clear to Georgette that her children did not understand the implications of what Herbert had just said about Robert, so she promptly clarified his remark: "Well, your father likes *men*." Her shame and disgust were obvious. Eric's initial shock and fear quickly escalated into "a homosexual panic."

While growing up, Eric had always been told by his mother that he was similar to his father in many ways, a comparison that usually felt good to him. Eric sensed their similarities as well: both are physically on the small side; both are "even tempered," "rational" rather than "reactive"; both tend to be somewhat distant, particularly in social situations. Because Eric was so much like Robert, did this mean that *he* was gay too? His confusion about this was to linger for many years. After the disclosure, Eric cannot remember any obvious changes that occurred in the father-son relationship: "My memory really goes blank after that." The most that he *can* recall is a kind of "anxious strain" between them.

Eric had been a good student throughout his early schooling, usually achieving As and Bs. Yet when he showed his first high school report card to his father, the response that came back—"Good," accompanied by a faint smile—was less than he had hoped for. Rose, more an underachiever, who routinely got Bs, Cs, and sometimes Ds, got a greater amount of unwarranted attention. Clearly, Robert's relationship with his son was different than the one he cultivated with his daughter. Over time, father and son grew further and further apart, reinforced by Eric's mother, who actively worked toward maintaining the growing split between them. Eric recalls "feeling very hungry for a connection with" his father, one he did not get then and has not gotten now.

Over time, Eric lost interest in school, dropping out in his senior year: "I had basically gotten into a place where I couldn't dig myself out anymore." In addition to what he perceived as his father's indifference to him, there were other problems at home contributing to his decision to leave. Georgette and Herbert had three more children together, all of whom were being neglected, making Eric and Rose responsible for "pick[ing] up a lot of the slack." Given Eric's anger about that, the fear he held for his stepfather, who seemed to constantly be in a rage, and the confusion about his own sexual identity, he accepted the offer to move in with family friends. They had a housewares business of which he enjoyed being a part. At the same time, he completed his GED. After doing some traveling and working a few odd jobs, he finally settled in New York City when he was twenty years old.

Upon his return to the area, Eric and his father started to see each other with greater regularity since they were "geographically closer." Weekly lunch engagements left Eric feeling "pleased," hopeful about the possibilities that lay ahead for their relationship, but pained too about the obvious distance between them, an emotional dilemma similar to the one he faced when he was four years old and his father came to visit for the first time after the parents' separation. "I think what came to be is the fact that we *were* different in ways that then I don't think we knew how to organize . . . into a relationship."

Eric sees those differences on a number of different levels: his father is politically conservative and Eric is a liberal; his father is "moralistic" and Eric is more accepting of others; his father tends to be highly "secretive," living a life of half-truths, and Eric is more open and revealing, trying to live the whole truth. How he attempts to negotiate those differences between himself and his father while still maintaining a connection with him will remain a lifelong challenge.

The setting for one of their weekly get-togethers turned out to be a local gay bar across the street from where Eric worked. On that occasion, Robert told his son that he was gay, a fact Eric had known for about seven years already. During that conversation, Eric acknowledged to his father that he himself felt "confused" about his own identity. Although he thought he was probably heterosexual, he had no experiences to really support it at that point. Shortly thereafter, he began to date women, "making up for lost time."

During this period, Eric tried to speak with his father about a romantic relationship he was having that was causing him some discomfort. Apparently the woman he was going out with was seeing another man besides Eric "and couldn't choose" between them. Robert looked at his son and said, "You know, [Eric], the gay lifestyle is . . . really wonderful. . . . It's so *free*." Although he realized his father was not necessarily "endorsing" homosexuality but rather just making some attempt to help him clarify what he thought was his confusion about his sexual identity, the remarks "alarmed" him. From then on, Eric recalls "getting together less and less" with his father. Added to this, Jack's "nuttiness" was surfacing in unexpected ways. He turned out to be a white supremacist who deeply hated blacks and Hispanics. He was also "heterophobic," toying sadistically with Eric, wondering when he was "going to come out and join them on the other side," obviously sensing his turmoil.

Before Eric was born, his mother told him that his father had said, "If it's a boy, I hope he's gay." Eric thinks that the source of the remark was Robert's retaliation against the mother about "the deal" he agreed to—"being forced to have a kid" in order to stay in their marriage—but it could also have been a wish for identification with a son. This mirrors Eric's wish for identification with a father, a still-unfulfilled need he has had his whole life: "I think there probably was a part of me that maybe wished I could be gay to be closer to him." At this point, Eric and his father are "more distant than ever"; more "muted" than ever. Their " 'occasion' relationship" requires that they get together on birthdays and holidays, joined by Eric's wife and Jack.

Eric's reactions to his father are always "mixed." He admires his father's musical accomplishments and his capacities as a teacher. However, the ways in which Robert and Jack have lived their lives— "picking up and . . . bringing home," in addition to involving other men in more permanent arrangements, either as friends or as lovers— shocks, angers, and disgusts Eric. It even makes him jealous at times. Further, Robert aligns himself with the right wing, for example, believing that gays should *not* be permitted to serve in the military. "Give a queen an inch, he'll take a mile" is his motto. Eric wishes his father could have more pride about being gay and be more like other gay men whom Eric has met both personally and professionally over the years, men who have had their share of problems but who nevertheless have managed to feel better about themselves.

On one hand, Eric is clear that whatever difficulties he had growing up and whatever regrets he now harbors are *not* all related to his father's homosexuality. Although it "did not help" and "added to a lot of confusion," particularly with regard to trying to sort out his own issues of sexual orientation, certainly his mother and his stepfather, both individually and collectively, contributed their share to the chaos. On the other hand, all of the problems Eric has gone through have now "become . . . the fabric, the texture, the complexity of life," which have shaped his choice of social work as a profession and which have allowed him to become the person he is.

Eric's relationship with Robert continues to be a tenuous one: "There's always an effort to find . . . pieces of my father." Cultivating connections with other gay men he admires is really a search for his dad, resulting in a sense of fragmentation. Although he remains doubtful that things will get better between them over time, Eric can and does strive to put all those pieces together by himself in the best way he can.

PAUL III

I can never forget . . . but I can forgive.

At forty-three years old, Paul III now looks at himself with pride. He has hurdled many obstacles and overcome many challenges. An "out-going . . . high energy, overachiever," Paul forcefully attacks life. He has completed a master's degree in business administration, has a managerial position at one of the largest corporations in the country, has been involved in a six-year committed relationship, has fathered and raised two daughters largely by himself, and now has joint custody and legal guardianship of three adopted sons. Life is good, but it hasn't always been.

Paul grew up in a well-to-do neighborhood just outside Pittsburgh. He is the oldest of three boys. One brother, Hank, is forty-one; the other, Jim, is thirty-nine. Their parents, Paul Jr. and Brenda, both sixty-three years old, were high school sweethearts, got married, then divorced eight years later. Paul was six at the time. His mother, he, and his brothers moved in with his maternal grandparents, who became the primary caretakers while Brenda worked. Paul Jr. lived with his own mother in the same neighborhood. During visitation with his father, Paul found out the reason for his parents' divorce. His dad was gay. He also had another secret: he was a pederast. On and off for the next thirteen years, until Paul was nineteen years old, father and son engaged in a sexual relationship.

What began innocently enough—touching, feeling, "fondling"—quickly escalated. His dad would tell him, "You can take your clothes off if you want. You're with me and . . . I love you." Oral and anal sex would eventually be part of their routine accompanied by pornographic movies used as instructional aids. It was their "big secret." A pact was drawn.

Over time, Paul developed a *dissociative disorder*. He was able to split himself off from what was happening in the moment. Before lovemaking, his father would routinely take off his watch and place it on the nightstand. Paul imagined leaving his body, going into the watch, and observing from there. Although this ultimately helped him to cope and survive that trauma, his own sense of identity became diffused in the process.

Just prior to the divorce, Paul III's mother met "Aunt" Chris. Their husbands served on the same police force. For many of the past thirty-seven years, the two women have lived, worked, and traveled the country together. Chris and her five daughters and Brenda and her three sons were all very much a family; they still are. Interruptions over the course of their relationship have occurred, however. Although Brenda was divorcing Paul Jr. when she and Chris first got together, Chris wanted to remain married to her current husband. Brenda, in a retaliatory move, got remarried to Richard five years later.

When Richard decided he wanted to adopt Brenda's sons, through some legal questioning, the details of the sexual relationship between Paul III, then age twelve, and Paul Jr. were finally uncovered in a lawyer's office. Everyone was "shocked." Because Paul Jr. did not want this to be public knowledge, he signed the adoption papers and waived visitation rights.

"Everything was wonderful" that first year. Paul III had hope again. He looked forward to a "Ward and June Cleaver-type life." Unfortunately, it was only the calm before the storm. His stepfather, a recovering alcoholic, "decided to pick up where [his] father left off." Physical abuse—a broken collarbone, a broken leg, chokings, beatings—and verbal abuse were tactics used to force Paul to submit to sexual relations with Richard. Paul began to act out and was sent to live in a military school for "incorrigible" youth. He never told anybody what was happening to him. Brenda, also an alcoholic and "a nasty" one at that, was having her own problems and remained emotionally unavailable, oblivious to what was going on under her own roof.

Although visitation rights had been taken away from Paul Jr., he continued to see his son while he was living at the military school and afterward. At fourteen, Paul started to work for his paternal grandmother's telephone answering service, and his dad would come to visit him. There, "in the back of her house," their sexual relationship continued. At thirteen, Paul was also having sexual relations with his mother's brother while residing with him one summer, *and* at fourteen with his father's brother. Although both uncles were married at the time, a history of relations between the men in the family, including Paul Jr. and his *own* father, was commonplace.

Why all this happened to Paul was and still is a mystery: "Was there some signal that I put off?" He was taunted at school as well. Always the shortest and smallest in his class, he was constantly called "fag" and "gay boy." Everyone seemed to be aware of something in him that he was never fully aware of in himself until many years later.

At sixteen, Paul got his driver's license; at seventeen, he moved out of the house, got an apartment with a friend, and found a full-time job; and at eighteen, after dating Marjorie for two years, he got married. He also had his last name changed back from his stepfather's to his original surname. When Richard got wind of this, he showed up at Paul's apartment and threatened him. Paul called the police and to this day twenty-three years later has never seen him again, literally shutting the door on one chapter of his life, opening it onto another.

Now a married man with a wife and two children, Paul had little contact with his dad, who had remarried and moved south. One afternoon while watching author John Bradshaw on Oprah Winfrey, someone on the show was discussing a history of sexual abuse. Paul had an awakening: "a lightbulb went off in my head." He had never thought of what happened to him as "abuse," never labeled it. It was just something that was part of life—*his* life, anyway. He immediately told his wife and they both decided he needed to get help right away. Paul was thirty years old at the time.

Over the next four years, through both intensive individual and group therapy, Paul got in touch with and then unleashed a tremendous rage. He also started to become more aware of the root cause of his own homosexual feelings, which he originally thought had more to do with the abuse rather than with him being gay. After all, *he* couldn't be gay; he was married and had children.

With his therapy now well under way, Paul decided to confront his father, blaming him because his "life was in the toilet." Getting word that his dad and his stepmother had been in a car accident, Paul took the opportunity to write a letter to him—a record of his memories and his feelings—and hand deliver it for maximum impact. It had been six years since father and son had seen each other. Face to face, they finally met.

PAUL III: Do you know why I'm here?

PAUL JR.: No.

PAUL III: I'm here to talk to you about my childhood and what you did to me.

PAUL JR.: What are you talking about?

PAUL III: Sexual abuse.

PAUL JR.: It wasn't so bad. You liked it. What's the problem?

With tears in his eyes, he handed his father the letter, got back in his car, drove north, and had no further contact with him for the next few years.

Consumed with trying to deal with all of this, his twelve-year marriage completely fell apart, although it had been shaky for years. His wife made it easy: she left. Paul was now a single parent, alone with two teenage daughters. Paul could not imagine his home without a mother for his children. So he went out and found one. Before the marriage, however, Paul had gotten a new job. One afternoon, a few of his co-workers invited him to go out for happy hour to the gay bar they all frequented. He agreed, although reluctantly: "They had me pegged." Standing there dumbfounded, having never met another gay person other than members of his own family, here at last were dozens of them—all gay, all acknowledging who they were, all feeling good about who they were. Paul was slowly coming to the realization that he was gay too. He called his marriage off.

In the meantime, Paul was reading everything he could on incest and on homosexuality. Over time, he came out to his ex-fiancée, his ex-wife, his best friends, and his two daughters. His father had apparently been doing some work on himself as well. He penned a letter a few years after that brief meeting with his son, noting that he regretted what he had done and begging forgiveness.

Since then, father and son have forged a new relationship, one based more on "friendship" than on blood. They have spent much time talking about what happened and why it happened. As Paul learned to forgive himself for the abuse, he has learned to forgive his father. He carried a great deal of shame about it, thinking that since he enjoyed it on some level it was his own "fault" that it occurred. He knows now that it wasn't: "It was the adult that was in control of that situation and not the child." He has no difficulty discussing all of this now. "I can never forget . . . but I can forgive."

He has no difficulty discussing his homosexuality now either. Paul is as much "out of the closet" as his father is *in* the closet. Certainly everyone in their family is well aware that his father is gay, having had a seven-year, live-in relationship with a man between his two marriages. However, it has never been openly discussed, except between father and son. Paul Jr. readily shares intimate details of his sexual encounters and his knowledge of gay Internet sites with both his son and with Michael, Paul's partner of six years. Despite the bond this creates, Paul also sees just how hypocritical his dad can be. He told his son for years to stay away from public sex but regularly engages in it himself—behind his wife's back, of course. Paul is perplexed and irritated by his father's desire to portray himself as "a wholesome upstanding citizen" and at the same time live a "double life." It is similar to his mother: although she has been in a lesbian relationship for much of the past thirty-eight years, she has never discussed her sexuality with her son, despite their commonality.

The shame and the guilt Paul once harbored about the sexual abuse pervaded his feelings about his homosexuality for many years as well. Although he now fully acknowledges that he is gay, Paul traveled a long way to get there: "I'm a Leo and I have . . . that need to be accepted." So when he did start to disclose, he was surprised that it didn't make a real difference to anyone he cared about and to anyone who cared about him. His chief concern: "Is this person still gonna like me and look at me the same way?" was easily assuaged. Now he says, "You couldn't shove me back in the closet if you tried."

Paul wonders what he would have been like had he not been sexually abused. It seems to have cast a dark shadow over everything. He could not separate his response to his father being gay from the experience of being abused, so intimately were they tied together, nor could he separate who his father was as a person. The "good memories" he has of the two of them going to amusement parks, going to the movies, and going to shopping malls are always tainted by the unspoken pact that these outings were a bribe for what was to come.

More important and not surprising, he had a great deal of confusion about his homosexual feelings. Many of his activities during young adulthood (getting married, having kids); the sheer quantity of the responsibilities he maintained in relation to his family, his school-ing, and his job; and the pace with which he kept it all up were all a defense against the possibility that he might be gay. He says with cer-tainty, "I . . . was keeping so damn busy that I didn't have time to deal with anything else."

Paul believes that at least he dealt with what happened to him in healthier ways than did both of his brothers, who were also abused by their father. One is a crack addict; the other is an alcoholic. Both re-fuse to have anything at all to do with their dad. Any contact they have at family gatherings is courteous but brief.

Paul sees himself as a survivor, the one in the family who has bro-ken the cycle of abuse. To him, "the glass is always half-full." He has the uncanny knack of taking "a sow's ear and mak[ing] it into a silk . . . purse." He feels that there isn't any situation that he couldn't handle now if so challenged: "If I can survive what I went through as a child . . . there isn't anything life could throw me that I couldn't survive." Al-though he fully acknowledges his past, he is determined not to "dwell in" it. For Paul, life is a continual challenge. Brimming with confi-dence, he says simply, "I've gone forward."

ELLIOT

He's probably more himself now than he ever was.

Growing up in a small, liberal, mostly white Ohio town has been a mixed blessing for Elliot. Although it was "perfect" in some ways—no crime, a strong sense of community—it was less perfect in other ways—everyone knew one another's business, which can work for or against you. Now twenty-six years old and attending graduate school in Wisconsin, Elliot goes back home several times a year, visiting all the good people who helped him grow up—those who "were there when [he] needed them and . . . [those who] are still there now."

His parents, Jill, age fifty-six, and Jonathon, age fifty-five, met while attending a church camp run by Jonathon's minister father. Jill's father is a minister too, so religion was important in both of their households growing up. Jill and Jonathon joined the Peace Corps a year apart and were both stationed in Malaysia, where they were mar-ried, before moving on to other parts of the globe, such as Germany and Japan. Their return home was accompanied by the birth of Elliot. Three years later his brother and "best friend" Jeffrey came along.

Religion continued to play an important role in the home they made together, particularly for Jill. She has spent a significant portion of her life devoted to the church and tried to instill its teachings in her children, much as her own father did and continues to do for her and for the rest of the family. At eighty-six, Jill's father is the family patriarch and although still quite "opinionated" he also brings a rational, benevolent, and calming presence to his family and his parishioners.

Although Jonathon too was involved in church-related activities when the boys were young, he had many other interests. "Weird as hell . . . incredibly eccentric . . . funny . . . very social," he is described by Elliot as a Renaissance man, a man for all seasons—a cook, a gardener, a decorator, a camper, and a carpenter. Always one to celebrate the common occasion by making things from scratch, he is the male version of Martha Stewart. A high school biology teacher by profession, his work life and his family life overlapped. Elliot and Jeffrey were "his students" by default, as he taught them about the natural world around them. Their lives would sometimes take on the quality of a biology lesson: hiking together, collecting plants and bugs together, caring for the animals they found every summer together, helping their dad prepare for the school year ahead.

Although he did "all the things dads are supposed to do," such as "play catch in the yard," for example, sports was never a real draw. Jonathon "never stood by the side of the pool with a stopwatch," never made his son feel like "a trained dog," as did other fathers he knew. The two shared many other interests. Elliot recalls that as a Cub Scout his dad helped him build a pinewood derby racer, then taught him how to put graphite on the wheels and attach weights in order to make the car heavier so that it would drive more quickly and smoothly. A good teacher, he allowed his son to do much of the work himself. Camping trips during the summer were always an adventure too. They slept in dome tents while on their way to some national or state park or point of historical interest, stopping at roadside tourist traps, such as the chocolate factory in Hershey, Pennsylvania, or the Corn Palace, or the Mystery Spot, just for fun. While mom was busy trying to cram their heads full of little-known but important historical facts, the brothers would amuse themselves by singing songs and playing games. Those early years seemed ideal in some ways: "everything was fine the way it was." His dad wasn't that different from other fathers; his parents weren't that different from other married couples. Both of them could be counted on to provide a strong, loving, and nurturing presence.

Elliot was privy to "the rumors" about his father, however. Yet other kids saying "Mr. [G's] a fag," didn't seem that big a deal since "every teacher [was] a fag or a bitch." That was just a fact of life. The idea that his dad actually *was* gay did not occur to him.

Unlike childhood, Elliot's early adolescence was less than ideal: "I was a geek and a little fat too." He spent time with his four boyhood friends, or with his brother, or by himself. He wondered what was wrong with him and wished that he were one of "the cool kids" and that girls were more attracted to him.

At around the time he started junior high school, Elliot became increasingly aware of "a weird tension" at home. His father began spending less and less time there. He routinely made trips to the neighboring city for "teachers' meetings," started exercising, lost weight, tanned, bought a used car, and was drinking more heavily. He was also constantly talking about people no one else in the family knew. During one visit with relatives, he became angered at a seemingly innocent "gay joke." These things were out of the ordinary for him: "We just knew something was wrong; something was different." Jill told her sons that their father was just "unhappy." Elliot considered it part of his dad's "midlife crisis," an attempt "to fight the aging process and hold on to his fleeting youth." Perhaps that was true, but other things were going on that Elliot was not aware of.

At the end of that summer, when Elliot was thirteen and about to enter the eighth grade, his whole family went to watch the fireworks display in the same city that Jonathon had been frequenting. During the festivities, a man walked by whom his father seemed to know. The two men chatted; Jonathon introduced Ben to his family, and they all decided to go over his house for a brief visit. It appeared that Ben was single—no kids, no wife—and had quite an odd assortment of "collectibles"—erector sets, toy trains. Elliot wondered how his father knew Ben and how he knew his house so well. The whole experience left him "a little uneasy" for reasons he did not completely understand.

The evening before school started, Elliot's dad told him he had to drive back to the neighboring town they had all just left a day or so before. Elliot didn't understand. Why would he possibly have to go there that night? Just as Jonathon was getting ready to leave, Elliot, furious with him, began interrogating him and asking him, among other things, why he had to go there the day before school. Then, more insistently, he asked if he was having an affair. His father did not respond. Upping the ante, he pressed him more forcefully, demanding to know if he was gay. "Yes, I'm gay," came the formal reply. Elliot doesn't recall the explanation his dad may have tried to give him at the time. He was crying and practically blocking the door, feeling like Luke Skywalker must have felt when Darth Vader finally "reveals that he is Luke's father." This just could not be. All the tension and all the events of the previous year quickly fell into place. Now everything made sense. Even so, he "wouldn't ever wish that moment upon anyone else."

Elliot does not completely understand what compelled him to ask his father that question. Clearly he was angry with him, not only for leaving that night but also for leaving so many times over the previous year, and lashed out with "the meanest thing [he] could have said." Dazed and confused, Elliot was also anxious and "scared," less concerned about the fact that his dad was gay than he was about the fate of their family. What was to become of them? "I felt like I lost my dad."

When he spoke with his mom that same night, he was equally surprised that she had known about her husband's homosexuality since the previous year. Over time, Elliot privately wondered why his father ever got married in the first place, why he decided to stay in it for so long, and why he stuck around for months after the disclosure. Elliot enlisted support not through his friends, who he suspects were already aware of his dad's situation, but mostly through the adults in his life—his guidance counselor Mrs. Autry, and John, a friend of the family, who turned out to be more helpful than the therapist he and Jeffrey saw together after their father told his younger son a few days after he disclosed to Elliot. In the weeks and months that followed, everyone in the community "knew." Such is life in a small Ohio town.

That year was a blur. How they spent Thanksgiving and Christmas is anyone's guess. His father was living with them part of the time, teaching at the same school, and living with Ben part of the time. Ben would remain Jonathon's companion for seven years. Elliot recalls trying to speak a bit more to his dad during that year, asking him questions about what it was like being gay, how you can tell if you are, and how you can tell if someone else was; he was attempting to understand something that felt very foreign to him. He also wondered about his own sexuality, questioned his religious beliefs, and considered more deeply the notion of marriage and issues of morality.

For Elliot, it seemed as though his dad was gay "all of a sudden." To complicate matters, the disclosure could not have come at a worse time for him. During early adolescence, issues of identity are central and loom large: "Trying to figure out who you are is bad enough, and worse if your dad is trying to figure out who he is."

After Jonathon made the break that year, finally leaving his fifteen-year marriage and moving in full-time with Ben, Elliot and Jeffrey would go to visit their dad. This became complicated. Ben, a painter and devoted dog lover, never really took a liking to the boys or perhaps was jealous of the time Jonathon spent with them. The feelings were mutual; they never cared for Ben either. To make matters worse, his house was a complete mess and not the least bit teen friendly. There was barely anywhere to sit, nowhere to sleep, and, worse yet, it reeked of "turpentine and old dog." So, much father-son time had to be spent doing things outside the house, some of them enjoyable, such as movies and projects; some of them "forced," such as going to PFLAG (Parents and Friends of Lesbians and Gays) meetings. All the people Elliot met there seemed "just incredibly uncool." Because he wasn't feeling particularly self-assured at the time, it didn't seem a good place to be. Clearly, it was a difficult transition for everyone.

One thing that remained constant over the years has been Elliot's relationship with his brother Jeffrey. "Always there for each other," they were close enough in age and close enough emotionally to be able to go through this experience together. Even though Elliot felt that his parents coddled Jeffrey more than they did him and that his brother got more of what he wanted more of the time, those slight jealousies did not seem to interfere in their relationship.

When Elliot was in high school, things got a bit better all around. He grew into himself physically—lost some of his baby fat, started to play tennis and soccer, and was in the best shape ever. He grew into himself psychologically too—"I knew who I was." Jonathon visited them frequently. He came to the games, the tournaments, and the band concerts, seeming to enjoy being there and watching his son's accomplishments.

As "the awkwardness of adolescence wore off," as Elliot continued to develop as a person, his dad was developing right along with him. After an extended period of experimentation, of trying to find ways "to fit in" with his new gay social circle and with his new sense of himself, Jonathon had no more need for that: "He's finally who he wants to be." The earlier flamboyance, a bit embarrassing to Elliot, diminished, or maybe Elliot just became more accustomed to or accepting of it.

Their similarities, obvious all along, have intensified with the passage of time. Both share an interest in the natural world; both share a distinct humanitarian bent. Elliot served in the Peace Corps—as did his dad—and is now studying ecology and teaching a class in plant identification—like his dad. They also share a disillusionment with religion and a similar political ideology.

They have become increasingly open about their feelings too, something that was difficult to do while growing up. At that time, working on projects together took the place of any real emotional exchange. Now they can freely discuss anything and everything. Elliot talks about his relationship with his girlfriend Emma, and Jonathon talks about his relationship with his companion Jay. Elliot thinks that both he and his father have matured and grown into themselves much more over the last couple of years and, as a result, their relationship has grown and expanded into a friendship.

Elliot continues to be concerned about his mother, however. He sees *her* as being the one who was most affected by all this. Since the divorce twelve years ago, she appears to be exclusively focused on her work and volunteer activities. To be sure, Jill and Jonathon continue to be friendly, catching up during family gatherings and supporting each other's common interests and activities. "Sometimes I still think my parents are together," Elliot says with some surprise.

About his father, Elliot concludes, "He's probably more himself now than he ever was." Even though he knows how hard it must have been for his dad to do what he had to do and how hard it was for the rest of them not to have him around, Elliot realizes that it was something that had to be. That doesn't change the fact that they're all very much "still a family"—maybe a different kind of family, but a family nevertheless.

THOMAS

I accepted him as he was.

Thomas was born in El Salvador twenty-two years ago. His parents—Edwin, age fifty-two, and Donna, age fifty—both grew up there. His grandparents were acquaintances too. Because the white Jewish community was a small one, everyone in it knew one another. Thomas's paternal grandfather, Hector, owned the local music store as well as organized many of the local cultural events. On one occasion, Hector was teaching his future in-laws, Donna's parents, how to play bridge. Apparently, the two didn't catch on fast enough for him and Hector lost patience. *"Pendejos"* [stupid], he barked, effectively ending "any chance of close relations—as well as the bridge lessons."

Edwin and Donna were not similarly deterred. Although they were childhood friends, they didn't see that much of each other during adolescence. Edwin attended junior high and high school in Canada, went to college in Babson, worked in Germany, and then came back home to run a coffee plantation, where the two met again. A few years later, "taken by the dashing young" Edwin, Donna married him.

Similar to his father, Thomas has seen much of the world. After the revolution in El Salvador began, Edwin and Donna took their son, then only one year old, and their daughter, Beth-Anne, then three years old, to Cleveland to live. A few years later his father's business necessitated a move to Belgium. While there, Edwin and Donna separated after a thirteen-year marriage. However, all of them continued to live together, albeit in different parts of their mansion, for the next year, until Donna decided to finally move out and take the kids with her. Although she got custody, Edwin got visitation rights in an out-of-court settlement—lunch during the week and sleepovers every other weekend. This arrangement lasted six years.

It was those lunchtime get-togethers during the first part of this period, when he was ten through twelve years old, that bring back some good memories for Thomas. There, around the table, he would routinely get "quizzed," not only by his dad but also by his paternal grandfather, who had moved in with them. "A young nerd," who was "keen on facts and statistics" like his dad, they would all "get along grandly" at those moments. The "competitive spirit" was alive and well.

It was during that period of his life that Thomas recalls looking up to his dad and idealizing him in a certain way, thinking of him as God: "He seemed to know everything, and I adored that about him. I too wanted to know everything. In that respect, I wanted to be like him." His tall, good looks added another dimension to the appeal. In another way, however, all those qualities made him seem unreachable and the prospect of being like him unattainable: "I felt that it was a mere fantasy that I'd ever be his equal."

The attention he got during the lunchtime quizzes was unusual, however. For much of his life, Thomas felt mostly ignored by his father: "I do not feel that my dad took a sufficient interest in me." Although his father represented God, he also represented Satan—a man who forced his son to do things against his will, embarrassing him in order to "make [him]self feel superior," which was entirely "unacceptable."

Although their relationship has had its ups and downs over the years, through it all Thomas held a consistent image of his father. The consummate businessman, Edwin is extremely bright, hardworking, competitive, money conscious, and "very sociable." Through his ingenuity, he has acquired a wide range of other skills, such as auto repair and gardening, which serve him well day to day. Never one to waste time, he also tries to actively discourage that tendency in others. Edwin thinks that things should be a certain way—his way. So, for example, if his favorite dessert doesn't happen to be on the menu, "he will order it anyway to make a point."

Conservative in his thinking, judgmental in his opinions, Edwin wields his ideas like a knife, demonstrating an unusual capacity to "convince anyone that their wine is really vinegar." Right after his parents were married, for example, Edwin forbade Donna to eat chocolate, trying to protect her from whatever property was in it that had given her migraine headaches. One day, she decided to do what she wanted. After buying a box then sneaking a piece, Donna suddenly heard her husband's footsteps nearby. Feeling nervous and guilty, she dropped the whole thing on the floor. In her haste, she failed to put all the pieces back in their original places. Edwin later inspected the box, realized what she had done, and was furious with her for going against his wishes. It was incidents such as these that led to the end of their marriage.

Thomas sees his dad as always needing to be the center of attention. Although this makes him appear "indestructible," it also makes him extremely dependent on the opinions of others and thus more vulnerable than he actually seems on the surface. Although Thomas is more inclined to focus on his father's more negative traits, at the same time he recognizes how "generous" he can be toward his family and friends. However, wanting appreciation for his generosity can sometimes spoil even this quality.

When Thomas was about fourteen years old, his father decided that he wanted to spend more time with his children and stopped paying alimony until an agreement could be worked out with Donna. After several months, Thomas and Beth-Anne split their time equally between their mother and father. Not too long after that, Edwin's business failed and he could not afford the payments, so the kids went back full-time with their mother, who now had an Israeli boyfriend living with her. After Donna and her boyfriend decided to move to Israel together the following year, Thomas was given the choice of where he wanted to live. He chose to stay in Belgium with his dad through high school. His sister had already made a decision to live and study in Israel, coinciding with the mother's plan. So the three of them went there together.

During adolescence, Thomas's extracurricular activities and social network expanded. He joined the Jewish scouts and was a member of the water-polo team. Therefore, as with most adolescents, his relationship with his parents took a backseat. Nevertheless, feelings of dislike and distrust predominated toward his father. Just as he started to think that there was a possibility they might be able to get along better, this feeling easily fell apart, like a house of cards. He wondered, "Why could others not see him the way I saw him?"

Just prior to all of this, however, in the summer of 1992, when Thomas was thirteen, he had a kind of epiphany: "I suddenly woke up and the first thing that entered my head was 'my dad's gay.'" Because this was such an unusual experience for him, it highlighted just how right the idea seemed.

In the spring of that year, Thomas had become more aware of a relationship his father, then forty-three, was having with another man, then twenty-one. Although he realized at some level that the young man never left his father's home, even "when night fell," Thomas had yet to "put two and two together." He doesn't believe he was denying reality. Somehow his dad being gay didn't quite fit: "He had kids, after all."

But waking up on that fateful morning with the idea that his dad was gay somehow *did* fit and "explained so many things"—the reason why there hadn't been women in Edwin's life after the divorce, the presence of the men who lived in their mansion, even the purple silk jackets his father wore. Just to confirm what he already strongly suspected, he asked his mother about it a few hours later. Donna admitted that his father was gay, a fact that relieved Thomas more than upset him: "I was so happy to finally understand things." He even laughed about it to himself.

Apparently Donna didn't find out about it herself until well after the divorce. Thomas thinks it wasn't Edwin's homosexuality that contributed to their split. Instead, he says, it was "because my dad was a bastard." Beth-Anne had been aware of their father's homosexuality two years prior and never said anything about it to her brother. Apparently, she had deduced it from reading a novel about a gay man and his daughter, recognizing in it many aspects of her relationship with her father.

Although Thomas has spent time talking with his mother and his sister about his dad being gay, at least in passing, he has never really spoken to his dad about it: "I could never share my thoughts and emotions with him." His father had never asked. Although Edwin was aware that Thomas knew, there was no father-son exchange regarding the matter until four years later, when Thomas was seventeen years old. On that occasion, Edwin's ex-partner, who was having dinner with Edwin and Thomas, initiated the discussion, asking Thomas how he found out and how he had reacted to it at the time. Edwin was more a bystander, listening to what his son had to say but not participating. Whether his dad had prearranged for his friend to inquire about this was unclear. In any event, Thomas felt very open to discussing it, prearranged or not. His attitude about it then and now: "Never for even half a second have I been perturbed by my dad being gay. . . . I accepted him as he was."

However, Thomas rarely disclosed the fact to his friends during this time in his life. Since he lived in a rather small community, he felt he needed to protect himself and was fearful that others would use the information against him. A few years later he told his girlfriend and his best friend, but only because they asked him about it first. Although all his current friends now know, it is never a topic discussed at length.

After high school, Thomas lived with his mother in Israel for a year and then moved to London, where his father was residing. Having recently completed college, he is now temporarily working for a trading company and living with his father and Don, Edwin's current partner of three-and-a-half years. In contrast to his relationship with his father, Thomas always got along well with his dad's three long-term boyfriends. One relationship lasted four years; the other lasted two years. Don is special, according to Thomas. Easy to talk with, humorous, and intelligent, Thomas thinks "that all signs point toward [Don] being *the* one." Don has been very much a parent to Thomas from the very beginning and even contributed to his college tuition.

Edwin's homosexuality "has always been a nonissue for" Thomas, more "another test of tolerance, a lesson in life on how everyone should be free to pursue their own thing." It makes no real difference to him if his father is with a man or a woman. Why would it? He pinpoints the origins of his attitude to a preoccupation with death. As a young boy, he recalls his sheer terror of going into the ocean, fearing the possibility of encountering sharks, alligators, crocodiles, or worse, all three. Although over time he eventually learned to better manage these specific fears, the idea "that one day we will all die" remains with him and colors his perceptions of the world. Add to the mix a young man who is staunchly atheist, combine this with overall "indifference" to most things, "and presto," you have Thomas, someone in pursuit of pleasure and creative expression—by playing his guitar and writing fiction mostly. This is a stark contrast to his father, someone in pursuit of status and money.

Although the fires of his smoldering rage toward his father have begun to cool in the past few years, they flare up every now and then: "I find it hard to look him in the eyes. . . . I hardly ever do." Now, as adults, man to man, the building blocks of their current and future relationship must ultimately rest on the compatibility of their personalities. Though "things aren't so bad," Thomas sees their extreme differences in outlook and temperament as getting in the way of forging a sense of intimacy, for right now anyway. Thomas is more focused on his own individual future, particularly the prospect of seeing his novel finished and published. What the future holds for his relationship with his father, only time will tell.

MATTHEW

I'm proud of *you* now.

Matthew's parents, Dan and Laura, met and fell in love as seniors at a small Christian college in Washington state. Before they married, Dan disclosed to his wife-to-be that he was gay. Times being what they were, both of them thought "that this was something that could be overcome; this was something that could be cured." All he needed was "the right woman." It didn't work. Dan was never "cured" and Laura never felt quite "right." So, after thirty years, they divorced. Now both fifty-five years old, they lead separate but overlapping lives, sharing two adult children—Matthew, age twenty-seven, and Michelle, age twenty-eight.

Dan was raised a Quaker in a small Oregon town. He tried to instill in his own children the sense of religious reverence and fervor that he had cultivated as a child. He not only enjoyed going to church, he depended on it spiritually and emotionally. It was the only "place where he felt somebody loved him." It gave him a reason for living, a reason for being. It defined him as a youth; it now defines him as a man. Matthew himself was actively involved in the church, too, as a young boy, although that was to change radically in adolescence. He attended "Christian camp and . . . was saved multiple times." He would wrap himself around his father during the service, fall asleep against his shoulder, or "walk out arm in arm" afterward. Other churchgoers observed and commented on their obvious closeness: "You guys seem just so comfortable together." Religion was a part of their day-to-day lives, too, even in play. Matthew recalls being permitted to use only the faceless, innocent-looking Rook cards as opposed to the regular deck of cards, which supposedly had their origins in the tarot.

Religion was not the only thing that brought father and son together in those early years of their relationship. Spending time outdoors infused Dan with life. Whether he was raking leaves in their yard, putting up a basketball hoop in the driveway, or building a deck out back, he tried to involve Matthew. Camping together, either as a family or just the two of them, provided memorable times as well, particularly skinny-dipping, a favorite pastime for Dan, who encouraged his son to indulge. Long walks set the stage for many special father-son moments. During one of those moments, Dan asked Matthew, then age thirteen, "if [he] ever touched [him]self," emphasizing that it was normal and natural and something about which he should not feel ashamed. This opened up a dialogue between them. Sexuality was now a subject similar to any other. In turn, Matthew felt that he could ask his father questions about his own sex life and "out of that came a real intimacy, a real bond." Dan revealed certain things about himself but *not* everything. The full story was not to come until ten years later.

Although his father's sense of openness and play could be infectious at certain times, it was also a cause for concern at other times. Not only would he defensively try to use it to get himself out of a tight spot when others confronted him—saying to them for example, "Let's forget about that and let's just go have fun"—it was also a point of difference between father and son. Matthew felt that while Dan was naturally playful, he himself was not. Matthew, now a computer software engineer, always felt temperamentally closer to his mother, a high school French teacher, than he did to his father, a former county commissioner and city planner. "The computer-geek-bookworm" was a part of Matthew that his father, more community and athletically minded, respected but never quite fully participated in.

Their differences worried Matthew in another way, particularly at those times when Matthew felt like he wasn't enough of what his father might want in a son, unlike a more outgoing cousin, whom he thought his father might have preferred. To complicate this, there were times early in his life when Matthew did not see that much of his father, which planted the idea that maybe "he was having an affair." Always alert to that possibility, Matthew closely observed his father's response to other women, even their waitresses, thinking that he might come back later to the restaurant to run off with one of them and leave his family behind.

Matthew also had worries related to his mother. Because Laura felt inadequate in her relationship with her husband, who she always knew preferred men, she dedicated much of her life to teaching and her students. Since "she couldn't . . . be one hundred percent for" her husband, "she could be one hundred percent for them." As a result, Matthew always felt he was "in competition with her students for her affection and for her love." Subsequently, the threat of being abandoned by both parents has undeniably shaped him. He had to work hard at getting the emotional supplies he needed by living up to what he thought their expectations were. The reality was that they were happy with who he was *already*. During one particular conversation when Matthew was in college, one that turned into "an hour-long hug," he revealed to his dad his fears about not being the son he might have wanted. His father responded empathetically, enumerating all the reasons he was so proud of him, including his academic prowess, which resulted in having gotten into the college of his choice: "I was just his son and that was all I needed to be." Matthew's fears about that abated, at least for the time being.

It was during this particular conversation that Dan revealed to Matthew "that there was something he wanted to tell" him someday, "something . . . he was not proud of," something shameful. So, here it was! At last, his father was going to admit what Matthew already knew: "He's had an affair." However, Dan did not say what it was. So Matthew was left to ponder. Five years later at age twenty-three, after relocating to California and after he had began working and living a fully independent life, he and his dad went on another camping trip together. Just as they were about to leave, Dan asked his son if they could go for a walk. After strolling along the beach for a while, they sat down. His father said that there was something he had to say, something "very important." He told his son that there were certain times in life when "children need to become parents to their parents." Matthew braced himself. Finally, with great hesitation, sputtering it out, Dan said, "I'm—I'm not just a heterosexual." Matthew's knee-jerk response was, "That's great!" relieved that his father had not had the dreaded affair with a woman, but also amazed by how many steps there had been leading up to this moment and how difficult this moment must have been for him. Dan countered with, "No, no, that's not great." He was clearly ashamed but simultaneously feeling a strong sense of relief after so many conflict-ridden years.

For Matthew, the disclosure made all his previous memories of his father seem somehow "unreal," as if Dan had been an actor in a play *before* this moment with all his lines written and rehearsed, and all his gestures "choreographed"; he had cast Matthew as an actor in the drama without his knowledge or consent. Now, finally, "stepping out of character," he was unmasked, revealing himself for who he really was. Matthew was in a new world.

Dan's disclosure came at a pivotal point in Matthew's own development. Just prior to it, he had done a great deal of soul-searching and was reevaluating his whole belief system as it related to the church and its teachings, specifically about drugs and premarital sex. The transition was a difficult one because it also involved the breakup of a serious romantic relationship: "My whole map was changing." It was during this time of intense transition but still prior to his father coming out that Matthew was encouraged by a friend to go see the newly released Australian film, *The Sum of Us,* which revolves around the complex relationship between Jeff, a young gay man, and Harry, his middle-aged, liberal-minded, widower father, who live together in Sydney. So excited was he by the film and by the quality of the relationship between the characters that Matthew told his father after they viewed it together, "If I ever had a gay son, this is how I would want to approach it." His father replied, "What if the situation was different. . . . What if the son's father was gay?" That baffled Matthew: "I never thought a gay man would have children." Dan clearly needed to test the waters over the course of years before finally taking the plunge he so dreaded.

Even before that incident, Matthew recalls having a dialogue with Dan about whether he knew anyone who was gay. His father responded that he did.

MATTHEW: Really? Who? Who?

DAN: I'm not gonna tell you.

MATTHEW: Do I know any of them?

DAN: Yeah. They're actually closer to you than . . . you might expect.

If Matthew was at all aware of his father's homosexuality, that awareness was more "on a subconscious level."

These scenes and similar ones were replayed in Matthew's mind after his father came out to him. Initially, he saw his father's homosexuality as a way to explain some of those differences between Dan and most of the other dads he knew: "This is why my dad dressed very nicely and this is why my dad was very sensitive." Perhaps it also explained the unusual closeness the two shared. The pieces were beginning to fall into place.

They were also beginning to fall into place for his sister, Michelle. She and Matthew had never been close growing up. They feuded constantly. Some of the difficulties in their relationship may have been rooted in Matthew's feelings that she was slightly favored by their father at times. Michelle was temperamentally closer to him and had a more obviously "playful side" than did Matthew—a side that Dan identified with. She had been "daddy's girl." Dan even escorted his daughter to the prom. However, after their father disclosed to them about being gay, their brother-sister relationship seems to have flowered. She confided in Matthew her history of attraction to gay men, supported by the fact that all of the boys she had been interested in during high school turned out to be gay. This set the stage for talking about their own conflicted relationship over the years. They were finally able to do a great deal of reparation and become "much better friends" in the process: "I see more of her spirit and what a good person she is."

Matthew's relationship with his mother also improved. Laura had been unable to share this part of her life with anyone, so when the secret was revealed she was both relieved and sad—relieved that she was now able to openly relate some of her own memories and experiences and sad that it meant the life that she knew was coming to an end.

Dan had a great deal of his own sadness about leaving his wife and would frequently call his son to console him. Matthew would be emotionally available for his father in the same way he felt his father had been there for him: "He had done so many good things for me growing up that here was a chance for me to . . . repay that." But, sometimes Matthew feels that his father and his mother unknowingly place him in the uncomfortable situation of being their mediator, and he has to actively encourage the two of them to speak with each other rather than "through" him. Also, Matthew has had to reorient himself to his father being newly single and dating and all the awkwardness and trepidation that comes with that territory. So when Dan asks his son's advice about someone he is currently dating, what he thinks of the prospective partner, or how he should handle a breakup—"Should I talk to this person? What should I do?"—Matthew has had to opt out of giving his opinion either way: "I want him to pick the person that he would be most happy with, not have me as part of the equation." Matthew feels that he now wants to be less of a peer and more of a son.

The same year that Dan came out, Matthew marched in his local Gay Pride parade, and after that he joined COLAGE (Children of Lesbians and Gays Everywhere), where he befriended other gays and lesbians and other kids in the same situation. His own thirst for knowledge took a new form, now becoming a way to adapt to the unexpected. He had come a long way since high school when his attitude was: "Just as long as they don't hit on me, then that's fine."

Matthew was instrumental in encouraging his father to become more actively involved in gay life. Having been a public figure earlier in his career in his small town, Dan had many legitimate concerns about exposing this part of himself. More recently, he summoned the courage and joined a group called Soulforce, an organization that roots out ignorance and bigotry and tries to expand knowledge and tolerance for gays and lesbians within the religious community.

On one occasion when Dan, a country-western music enthusiast, was visiting Matthew during his city's Gay Pride celebrations, he took his father to a local bar where Dan was able to enjoy country-western dancing the way he did back home. Matthew's own introduction took an interesting twist. During the course of the evening, Matthew was approached by a guy, who asked *him* to dance. Although not really a dancer at all and not especially comfortable dancing with another man, he did it anyway, somehow managing to get through it. When the young man asked him why he was there, Matthew replied, "Oh, I'm here with my dad." His dancing partner was baffled.

Matthew feels that his father coming out has opened up a deeper level of communication and honesty in his family as a whole. All the other issues they face together now seem small by comparison. This "drama" has forced them all to look at themselves and each other in new ways. For Matthew individually, this experience has expanded his ideas about who gay people are and "the communities within the community." It has also taught him not to "assume" too much about anyone. Much to his surprise, he finds the same degree of homophobia and racism, particularly in the gay male community, as he sees everywhere else. On a broader level, whatever fears he might harbor about any unfamiliar culture he does not allow to stand in his way. He feels he is now more curious, more fearless, and "more gregarious" in relation to the wider world.

However, the picture is not perfect. There are drawbacks. Now that his father has moved out of the family home and into his own place, Matthew has to decide how and where he is going to spend his time when he goes back for a visit. Although his dad has done everything possible to make his home warm and comfortable, Matthew still prefers to stay where he spent twelve formative years in what is now his

mother's house. Soon there may be a new addition to the family—
Laura's fiancé. Accepting that reality has not been easy for him, either.

On a deeper level, Matthew can now see that keeping his father's
homosexuality a secret has been an inhibiting influence. For years,
his family seemed more socially isolated than most of the other families he knew. He didn't quite understand why that was and sought out
his friends' families to provide the contact he could not get from his
own. After Dan came out, his mother explained to her son that, typically, the closer you get to others, the more you are expected to reveal
to them. Because of her shame about her marriage to a gay man, she
did not want to expose that part of him and therefore tended to protect
herself by placing limits on her social contacts. Therefore as an adult,
Matthew has had to work against his tendency to isolate. On the contrary, the relationship he has had with his father has mostly been a
very open one, partially offsetting the secrecy that surrounded his homosexuality and the damaging effects that the secret caused.

Matthew is aware of the long and difficult road Dan has traveled
and will continue to travel, although he is still far from his final desti-
nation. Like his father, who has expressed pride in *him*, Matthew re-
spects his father for being honest with himself and for being honest
with those who love him. He wants him to know: "I'm proud of *you*
now."

Chapter 5

Findings

In this chapter, I compare and contrast the responding sons, breaking the interview material down into four categories: (1) *beginnings,* which covers the first memories of their fathers and the early years of their relationships spanning childhood and adolescence; (2) *suspicions* the sons had about their fathers' homosexuality prior to the disclosure; (3) the *disclosure* itself; and (4) the *impact* this has had, or not had, on the sons and fathers individually and together. As in Chapter 4, all quotations come directly from the interview transcripts.

BEGINNINGS

First Memories

He was holding me up while walking through a pool.

Shawn

For many of the sons, the first memory of their fathers was not always a clear one, nor were they always sure how old they were at the time; several memories may have converged at once, making it difficult to determine which one came first; or some memories may have been constructed from photographs or from what others told them, a common phenomenon, called a *screen memory.* Whatever first memories of their fathers they could summon, all were characterized in similar ways.

Shawn reports his first memory of his dad at less than a year old: "He was holding me up while walking through a pool." At two or three years old, Thomas remembers flying in the plane—"probably . . . a Cessna"—his father, a licensed pilot, had rented, "looking out the window . . . to the ground below and seeing a shoreline." Richard's first memory of his father was associated with him winning the rubber ducky race in which he split $10,000 with several other contestants after their rubber ducky crossed the finish line first: "That was pretty cool." He was three at the time. The first memory Noah recalls "cleanly" at about three-and-a-half is of him and his father finding a blackboard in the trash one day, taking it home, washing it, and then using it for practicing reading and math. At around the same age, Andy reconstructs this: "We are walking around the lake and I am holding his hand. I remember him being really tall."

For many of them, their first memories occurred a bit later. Rob, for example, remembers his dad showing him how his Dukes of Hazzard Power Wheels scooter worked. Matthew recalls raking leaves together with his dad. Two other memories converge for him at around the same time: watching his father put up a basketball hoop in their driveway and playing with a slide rule while sitting at his father's desk at work. He was around five.

One of Eric's first recollections was anticipating the meeting he had with his father several months after his mother forbade her husband to see their children. Between four and five years old at the time, he felt a mixture of excitement and anxiety as he heard his dad, "a bit of a stranger," coming up the steps to their second-floor apartment. Who was this man exactly?

Paul, then five or six, had a first memory of his dad lying in bed with him and his father expressing how much better it would feel if they didn't have any clothes on: "let's take ours off and get closer." He recalls feeling "confused, scared, yet very excited."

What may have been clearer at times were collective images and feelings rather than a particular memory. Joseph says, "I can't really pinpoint any specific memory," but he can recall his excitement when his father would come home from work and how he "would run up to him and hug him." Mark remembers all the time he spent with his dad during those early years doing the usual father-son things, such as trips to the zoo, and just how satisfying that felt to him, given their "very easy connection" with each other.

Elliot recalls the warm, yet bittersweet memory he had of his dad preparing breakfast every Saturday morning for their family: "We would wake up to the smell of bacon and waffles—the syrup usually warm . . . with blueberries or something like that on the side. We ate together very often, and Saturday morning breakfasts were pretty much a mainstay in our house." This occurred until he was twelve years old, about a year prior to his dad leaving their home.

So it seems that the fathers are, for the most part, initially recalled as loving men who, in a sense, lifted their sons up, brought them to a higher place, as Shawn's father literally did; they were men who wanted their sons to see life from another angle, to show them things they couldn't see themselves. Whatever tentativeness the sons may have experienced in trying to accurately recollect those first memories is left behind as they reconstructed with greater sureness the fathers of their early years.

Childhood

I really looked up to him.

Eric

The sons' experience of their fathers in childhood seemed to elaborate and expand on the themes of those first memories. Despite the continual geographical flux that took place early on in many of their lives, and despite the conflicts the parents may have been having during this time, the sons attempted to keep their relationships with their fathers as separate from those events as possible. Although some of them painted idealized portraits, certainly not all of these relationships were conflict free.

A few of the fathers spent much of their time at home when their sons were young, as did Mark's dad, John, a documentary filmmaker during that period. As a result, he had more time for Mark. Ideas were always the way the two of them connected. If they took a trip to the zoo, they would talk about where the animals came from; if they took a trip to the natural history museum, they would talk about dinosaurs and extinction. Having "a similar brain" led them down a similar path— history and facts of all kinds. As a youngster, the fights that used to go on between his parents were frightening to Mark. After the separation and after his mother received custody of her sons, they moved around the country, so Mark didn't see his father as much. Although in his own way he still felt close to his dad, he tended to feel more aligned and more protective of his mother, at least at that point in his life.

Noah's dad, Dennis, an actor during Noah's early years, waited tables between acting jobs. With little ability to tolerate the stress, he frequently got fired, which equaled more time at home with Noah. "He was sort of my primary . . . playmate," is how Noah describes Dennis, at least through age five. Subsequently, his parents separated and Noah had to find new playmates. After spending a year in California with his mother and her boyfriend, the three of them came back to New York where Noah would "yo-yo back and forth between" his parents, remaining as close to his dad as ever.

Rob's father, Warren, was also a "stay-at-home dad" who spent more time with his sons after his wife started law school and after he retired from the Air Force. Warren tried to be there for his son in whatever way Rob needed him to be: "He always taught me how to play baseball when I wanted to play baseball, even though I was never really any good at it."

Although Joseph's family didn't have the money and privilege that his Park Avenue friends were accustomed to, he never felt a sense of deprivation either. His dad, Ian, gave him the attention he needed—a gift for his birthday and a gift on the holidays and, on one occasion, he helped Joseph assemble the go-cart that turned out to be, among his friends at least, "one of the fastest ones."

Eric describes the early years with dad Robert as "absolutely wonderful." After his parents separated, Eric and his sister used to go visit their father and his lover every other weekend. From road trips to camping to the World's Fair to zoos to museums: "You name it. We . . . did it." Robert would also come to their home to give his children violin lessons. His gentle way infused his son with love for his father: "I admired him. . . . I really looked up to him."

Elliot's dad, Jonathon, created a sense of adventure for his two sons. A biology teacher by profession, Elliot and his brother were almost like "students." Hikes in the woods provided a natural setting to acquaint and attune them firsthand to nature. A jack of all trades, Jonathon could cook, garden, build, and decorate—sometimes involving his sons, sometimes not. Summer vacations were an annual event, providing yet another venue for learning and excitement.

Matthew, too, always had the experience of togetherness with his dad Dan. Whether in church, on a camping trip, taking Matthew to work with him, or just raking leaves in their backyard, Dan always tried to make his son feel he was an important part of his life. As a young boy, though, Matthew was preoccupied with the possibility that his father was having a relationship with another woman: "That was a big fear for me." The fact that Dan worked a great deal and was out of the house much of the time, combined with Matthew having seen the film *Mr. Mom,* in which some of the characters flirt with the idea of infidelity, made him suspicious of his father.

Richard and his father, Charles, shared many activities early on too—fishing, visiting friends and relatives, even grouse hunting. But before his parents were divorced four years ago, Richard recalls that period as the most difficult time in his life. Their "brutal" arguments were "pretty scary" for him.

Andy's parents separated shortly after their son was born. His father, Miguel, moved to Florida, where Andy would visit him. Miguel would share with his son what was, to Andy anyway, an idyllic life complete with a beautiful home, gardens, a waterfall, and about 100 finches. Trips to Sea World, Disney World, or the beach with his musically talented, charismatic, good-looking father added to the excitement.

In contrast to Andy's father, who was mostly physically absent but sometimes emotionally present, Shawn's father, David, was mostly physically present but sometimes emotionally absent during the early years of his son's life. Even though he spent much time teaching Shawn about music and supporting his talent, there was something missing. With his own parents as a model, David placed much importance on discipline, instilling "a healthy fear of God" in his son. The result was a dad who was more hands off than "hands on."

"At that time my dad represented both God and Satan to me" was how Thomas describes the father of his early years. On one hand, he idealized Edwin and longed to be like him in certain ways. His knowledge, intelligence, and good looks made him appear almost perfect in his son's eyes. On the other hand, Thomas rarely got the attention from him he thought he deserved. And when he did, it was the negative kind. His father would frequently embarrass him in order to get Thomas to do things he didn't want to do.

Although Paul has some good memories of his dad—trips to amusement parks, shopping malls, dinners, movies—those activities were usually a means to an end, that end being the sexual relationship his father cultivated with his son from age six. Indeed, all of Paul's childhood experiences with his dad were colored by the sexual abuse. Although "done in a very loving way . . . it was still . . . abuse," he acknowledges.

Adolescence

> My relationship with him didn't change. It just became more
> complicated.
>
> Elliot

In contrast to childhood, the period of adolescence is usually
fraught with more conflict between parents and their offspring. But
this was not necessarily the case for all of these sons. Rob is not aware
of any real changes in the quality of his relationship with his dad from
childhood through adolescence: "It was all the same. It didn't really
change." Noah echoes this. He says, "I think my relationship with my
father was pretty much the same." Even though both he and his dad
went through their own individual changes while Noah was in adolescence, there was a consistency about their relationship over time.
Although it is too early to say much about the adolescence of thirteen-year-old Richard and his dad, currently Richard describes his father as basically interested in and attuned to his son, despite the conflicts with Richard's mother. Paul's connection with his dad didn't
change much, either. It continued to be marked by the sexual abuse,
which continued unabated until Paul was around nineteen.

Shawn says that as he got to be a teenager, things actually got
better between him and his father. When he was eleven his dad, David, moved to San Francisco, where Shawn went to visit him every
summer and on selected holidays, an experience he found personally
fulfilling. He was exposed to a slice of life he never would have seen
in the Virginia town he lived in during the rest of the year. During this
time, Shawn describes his father as "a good balance between being a
summer buddy and an ever-present parent." Although David was
constantly *on* his son about things such as grades and appearance—
"It was a little stifling at times"—Shawn always knew "he was always there, always cared."

Matthew, too, thought that in adolescence he felt an increased sense
of intimacy with his father, Dan. Despite some differences, which
mostly revolved around Matthew's decreasing interest in church, father
and son cultivated "a real bond." He traced the turning point in their relationship to a conversation they had about sexuality. Things really
opened up between them after that. The fact that they could talk easily

about a subject as taboo as sex made everything fair game, even though Dan was still years away from coming out to his son or to himself.

Mark had a strong desire to get closer to his dad, John, during his adolescence, leaving his mother's home in California and relocating to his father's home in New York City: "I think I was at an age where that was . . . an appropriate and important thing to really sort of feel that connection." His hopes were high. But those expectations were harder to attain than he anticipated. Not only was he exposed to the problems John was having with his new family, but also his father was away on business much of the time. When he *was* home, he was hard to approach: "I spent a lot of my time as an adolescent feeling like I couldn't confront him or talk to him about anything."

Andy's trips to Florida to visit his dad, Miguel, were fun until about age fifteen. Miguel had worked hard for many years to bring his parents and sister to this country from Cuba, and he wanted his son to get to know them. However, the connection between Andy and Miguel's family never really developed. The time Andy spent with them he would rather have spent with his dad alone. So after that summer, Andy stopped visiting his dad because it just wasn't fun any longer. Also, his dad got progressively more ill over the next couple of years and couldn't be with his son in the same ways.

Thomas acknowledges being angry with his father for much of his life and "consumed with rage" during the better part of his adolescence. Since he could not get beyond those feelings, a healthier relationship was impossible at that point.

Joseph paints a rather dramatic shift in his relationship with his dad from childhood to adolescence. As his parents' relationship became more conflicted, their home became more riddled with tension. As his dad, Ian, became more frustrated, not only with his marriage but with his career, he would on occasion make Joseph the target of his anger. "Punishments" were routine. When Ian finally left home, Joseph, fifteen at the time, felt some relief but more rage at his dad for abandoning them. In the years that followed, he lived with his father part of the time and with his mother part of the time, feeling "very torn" between them.

Without getting too much ahead of sequence here, let me say that even though many of the sons became aware of the fathers' homosexuality either before or during adolescence, for some of them, especially Rob, Noah, Shawn, Thomas, and Richard, the effect of that knowledge on their relationships, according to them, was minimal at the time. Whatever the quality of their relationship before, it did not radically shift at the time the sons learned about their fathers' sexual identity, or afterward, for that matter.

In two other situations, however, the fathers' own difficulties with their homosexuality and/or the disclosure had more of an effect on the relationship during this time. It was impossible to separate them. Elliot illustrates this point:

> My dad's coming out was kind of all lumped in there with my adolescence. I mean that when someone asks me to give them the defining moment of junior high, I'd say, "Well, my dad told me he was gay the weekend before eighth grade started." I guess my relationship with him didn't change. It just became more complicated.

His dad, Jonathon, split his time between households until he moved in with his companion, Ben. Although he remained a very active part of his son's life, Jonathon's disclosure was clearly a disruption.

The same was true for Eric. After his mother revealed to her thirteen-year-old son that his dad "like[d] *men*," the shock and fear sent him into a tailspin. But he cannot clearly pinpoint if there was, in fact, a shift in his relationship with his father. His says his memory "goes blank" right after. The "anxious strain" between father and son, present to some degree throughout much of his early life, was the result of many factors. It was partly orchestrated by Eric's mother, who didn't trust her husband with their children; partly by the character of his father, who couldn't get too close emotionally to his son; and partly by Eric, who was in a homosexual panic during much of this period, fighting the possibility that he might be gay himself.

SUSPICIONS

I've kind of had this suspicion.

Andy

Awareness of their fathers' homosexuality existed at different levels prior to the actual disclosure. Two sons said they were not aware at all, seven were subliminally aware (DeVine, 1984), and three were consciously aware.

In the first category was Joseph who, despite being gay himself, reported absolutely no inkling at all about his dad, Ian. At around age twenty, when he showed up for a party at his father's place accompanied by his boyfriend, he found Ian there with *his* boyfriend. Ian had never revealed this to his son before. Although he had lived the life of an artist in which, stereotypically anyway, sexuality could be "ambiguous," as far as Joseph knew, all of his dad's partners after the separation from his mother had been women. Similarly, thirteen-year-old Richard reported no awareness that his father was gay before being told by him a couple of years ago, well after his parents separated.

Seven of the sons were aware, at some subliminal level, of the possibility that their fathers might be gay. Yet even within this category there were many gradations, from those less aware to those more aware.

As a young boy, Eric spent every other weekend with his dad, Robert. Waking up early one morning, he recalls

> looking at my father and his lover . . . and having this sort of curious thought, that was probably [a] very quick flash, about the fact that they were two men living together. And that seemed different to me in some way. But then I remember sort of dismissing it pretty quickly. But it had stayed with me. And so I don't know if that was sort of a recurring curiosity that would come and go at different times.

As a preteen, Shawn recalls having some vague suspicions too. After the separation, his father moved near Dupont Circle in Washington, DC, a locale that Shawn read somewhere had a large gay population. Also, his mother started to date but for some reason his dad didn't: "I think that I was a little scared of the truth." Mostly he was concerned about what his father being gay would mean in terms of himself. He was already "relentlessly teased" by the other kids, mostly because he was overweight. This would just give them more ammunition.

Perhaps a bit clearer than Shawn was Rob, who says he suspected his dad might be gay, partly because Warren seemed to have no interest in women after his parents separated. These suspicions increased when he stumbled upon his dad's briefcase during a game of hide-and-seek. After opening it and finding it filled with gay pornography, his response was, "Huh, OK." His mom had already come out to him, so anything was possible. But how likely could it be that both of his parents would be gay? He "dismissed it."

Although Matthew says, "I don't consciously remember wondering if my dad was gay," his preoccupation with the possibility of both his parents having affairs was, perhaps, a signal that he intuitively felt there was something amiss in the relationship between them. Interesting, too, was that while in college, Matthew took his father to see *The Sum of Us,* the Australian film about a father and his gay son, because he had heard from a friend that it was a great story "about a great relationship." During their conversation about it afterward, Dan asked Matthew how he thought a son should handle it if his father was gay, the reverse of the situation presented in the film. Matthew says, "I didn't have an answer for that." He says that any awareness at all on his part was purely "subconscious."

Similarly, Elliot says of himself as a preadolescent, "It literally never crossed my mind that my dad could be gay." Although privy to what the other students in school said about his father, a teacher there, namely that "Mr. [G's] a fag," he didn't consider it seriously. The first thing that alerted him was Jonathon's anger at "a gay joke" that either he or his brother made: "I remember being told to never say anything like that again." Around the same time, Elliot observed his father changing radically—he was exercising, losing weight, tanning, drinking more than usual, and was gone from the home more. All of this came to a climax when Elliot finally confronted his dad, demanding to know if he was gay. "I guess I just put a few things together," he acknowledges.

Mark's mother told her thirteen-year-old son that he "didn't really know who [his father] was" at the point when he started to talk about the possibility of going to live with his dad. True enough. That was why he wanted to live with him in the first place. After his mother hinted something about John having relationships with other men, a "big weird . . . cloud" loomed over him for quite some time. Mark didn't quite understand what she was getting at and wanted to ask his father about it. But he clearly read the message that it was all "some dark secret." When he finally got up the courage to talk with him a few years later, John minimized the whole thing, saying "he had experimented . . . and . . . that wasn't really who he was." Mark happily accepted it.

By the time Andy reached adulthood, he had pretty much put the pieces together about his dad, who had been a hair stylist, a bird collector, and whose "best friend" was a flight attendant. He had also died of AIDS ten years ago, something his aunt confirmed after Miguel's death. Although Andy had tried to dismiss the possibility at age seventeen, saying to himself there was "no way" that could be true, right before he got married, he wanted his fiancée to know his thoughts. He said to her:

> I've kind of had this suspicion. And I don't know if it's true . . . [but] someday we might find out that my dad was gay. How would you feel about that? . . . Would that bother you?

Finally, there were three sons who had no doubt at all about their dads' sexual orientation before the disclosure. Noah describes himself as always alert to what was going on around him, even as a kid. When his parents separated and he started to hang out more with his dad, he recognized that many of his dad's friends were gay. One day, while going through his father's closet for stuff to play with, Noah inadvertently stumbled upon some gay pornography: "That pretty much sealed the deal."

At age thirteen, Thomas had an epiphany. He even remembers the exact day—July 25, 1992:

> I suddenly woke up and the first thought that entered my head was "my dad's gay." Maybe my brain was working with fits and starts, and that it might have been denying something that should have been apparent weeks before. But I don't believe in a subconscious . . . so I don't buy the denial business. . . . I just did not think that it fit that my dad was gay. He had kids, after all.

His father's homosexuality, however, would explain "so many things"—the presence of the other man who lived in their mansion, the absence of women, not to mention the fashion choices, such as purple silk jackets.

Even though Thomas says he didn't "buy the denial business," clearly denial did act as a defense for him and for many of the others against the possibility, the danger (Freud, 1966) that their dads were gay. For Paul, there was no denial. The sexual relationship he had with his father since the age of six said it all.

DISCLOSURE

So, what's for dinner?

Shawn

The Context

The precipitating factors that pushed the fathers to disclose to their sons were not always clear. At times, the sons themselves exerted some pressure. Wanting to lift the "dark cloud" around his mother's intimations about his father, Mark initiated a dialogue with him. But John couldn't tell him the whole truth at the time, although he finally did about eight years later. Elliot confronted his father very directly during the height of an argument, demanding to know if he was gay.

Mostly it seemed the fathers waited until they were ready themselves. Whatever pressure they felt came from inside them, rather than from outside. They also waited until they thought their sons would be able to comprehend what it meant to be gay *and* be able to emotionally accept what it meant for them to have a gay father. (The notable exception to this was Paul's father, whose own sexual and emotional needs took precedence over his son's.) Their readiness usually occurred after most had either begun the process of separating from their wives or had already separated. (Mark's father was in the middle of separating from his second wife.) A few were already in a gay relationship. (Paul's father had separated from his first wife, then had a relationship with a man for about seven years, and has now been remarried to another woman for the last twenty-five years. According to Paul, however, his father still identifies himself as gay.)

The sons learned about their father's sexuality at different ages: Noah and Paul found out as children; Richard and Shawn found out as preteens; Elliot, Rob, Eric, and Thomas found out as teenagers; and Joseph, Matthew, Mark, and Andy found out as adults.

For some of them who learned about it at a younger age, particularly Shawn, Elliot, Richard, Eric, and Paul, it threw into question their own orientation. Although they may have wondered about it anyway, the knowledge of their father's homosexuality most likely made them self-examine more than they might have. (For Paul, the question of his sexual orientation was complicated by the abuse.)

Most were first told by their fathers; Mark and Eric were first told by their mothers, then later by their fathers; Thomas was told only by his mother; Andy was told only by his fiancée.

In most cases, there was a tremendous reluctance for the fathers to verbally disclose. This was evidenced in many different ways. On one end of the continuum was Andy's dad, Miguel, who died before he told his son. Edwin has never had a discussion with Thomas, even though Thomas has lived with his father and his father's partners off and on for many years. Paul's dad, in effect, disclosed to his son through his sexual acting out.

As noted, Eric and Mark heard something about their dad's sexuality from their mothers first. The ways in which they told their sons— their words, their tone—made their shame and their disgust all too obvious. Both boys had fuller discussions with their fathers years later.

Most of the fathers who chose to disclose did so with great reticence. Matthew's father, Dan, did it in stages. He laid the groundwork years before, telling Matthew at that time there was something he wanted his son to know about him, something "he was not proud of." But it would have to wait. Five years later, practically choking with fear, he finally said it: "I'm—I'm not just a heterosexual."

Mark found out in bits and pieces. His dad, John, initially denied he was gay after Mark asked him but finally revealed himself about eight years later in the context of a family meeting. Elliot's father introduced his sons to his partner, Ben, without telling them who Ben *really* was. A couple of days later, Elliot confronted his father with the truth, even though he didn't completely know it *was* the truth at the time. Ten-year-old Noah had to gently coax it from his dad, until he finally said, "Well, I mean, do you want me to say that [Ron] and I are lovers?" Joseph had never had a discussion with his father before showing up at a party where he found Ian and his boyfriend being affectionate. On the other end of the spectrum were Rob's, Shawn's, and Richard's fathers, who all told their sons openly and directly and who all seemed to encourage a dialogue about it.

Immediate Responses

The sons' first responses to their fathers' sexuality produced a range of feelings. On the furthest end of the continuum was Noah, who at ten years old was indifferent to it, considering it a nonissue, anticlimactic, something he had already known for close to two years, and something he had already informed some of his friends of several months earlier. He describes his father as more anxiety ridden about it than he had been.

Relief was the predominant feeling for Thomas, Shawn, Matthew, Rob, and Andy. Thomas "was so happy to finally understand things." Shawn's first words were, "So, what's for dinner?" experiencing "a certain peace that comes from knowing the truth." Matthew's first response was "That's great!" He was thankful that Dan had not had the affair with a woman he had dreaded all along. He also felt a sense of awe that his father had found enough courage to finally face this and tell him. Rob's suspicions were confirmed, saying to his dad, "All right, we kind of . . . had our own thoughts that you were," referring to his brother and himself after they were told together.

Although Andy initially expressed relief too, reflected in his statement, "OK, I'm glad I know for sure," he then entered a new phase, one characterized by feeling angry, not only with his dad but also with the other members of his family for not telling him the truth about who his father was: "It hurts to say I am angry at my dead father or angry at my poor deprived mother. But I am. I am very fucking angry. . . . I don't care that my dad was gay. I care that nobody told me!"

Mark had different feelings all along the way. After his mom hinted something about John and his relationships with other men, Mark felt confused; when he approached his dad a few years later and his father said he wasn't gay, Mark felt relieved. When the formal disclosure finally came eight years later, one that he had anticipated moments before his father actually said the words, whatever shock he felt quickly escalated into anger about "being lied to for so long." Similar to Andy's reaction, the disclosure felt like a betrayal to him, a failure of trust between father and son when Mark had been searching for the truth about his father for so long.

Joseph said, "It was surprising but not shocking," the day he saw his dad with another man. Richard felt a bit shocked and a bit fearful about what others, such as his family and friends were going to think.

On the more extreme end was Elliot who says he "wouldn't ever wish that moment upon anyone else." As his father was getting ready to leave the home to visit the nearby city where his partner, Ben, lived, Elliot began asking his father why he was leaving—again. Was he having an affair? Was he gay? When the truth came, it knocked him over. Dazed and confused, he thought to himself "it couldn't be true."

After Eric's mother told him that his "father likes *men*," her shame and disgust filled him with shock and fear. Being so much like his dad in so many ways, Eric wondered if this meant that he, too, liked men. A homosexual panic ensued that lasted for years. Suicidal feelings and fears about going to hell were close to the surface. Eric didn't talk with his father about this directly until seven years later, when he was around twenty years old. Sitting in a gay bar across the street from the restaurant where Eric worked, Robert finally told him. In turn, Eric told his dad that he already knew. Eric also revealed that, although he thought he was "basically . . . heterosexual," he had been grappling with some confusion about his own sexual identity for quite some time.

For Elliot and initially for Eric, the knowledge of their fathers' homosexuality appeared to create a crisis for them, that state in which there is a sense of falling apart, a sense of disequilibrium, a danger, a time when one is up against a new situation that calls for a new solution (Parad and Caplan, 1965; Rapoport, 1965). Elliot's immediate anxieties were centered more on the meaning of this for the future of his family; Eric's were centered more on the meaning of this for him as a sexual being.

Paul's situation was very different. Since it was *not* his father's homosexuality per se that created problems but rather the acts of sexual abuse, it would be impossible to sort out a response to a disclosure, if that's what one would call it in this case. He does recall much fear, confusion, and excitement about being with his father in a sexual situation.

IMPACT

> Not all of this is about sexual orientation. . . . This is about my
> father.

Eric

As I observed earlier, disclosure is a contextual act. In understanding its effect, I will look at: the sons' perceptions of their fathers, any changes they have seen in the father-son relationships, any changes they have seen in their fathers individually, and any changes the sons see in themselves resulting from the disclosure.

The Distant Father

In exploring the sons' perceptions of their fathers, there was an obvious commonality: the distance their fathers maintained from them, although the causes of this varied widely. In certain cases, that distance was confined to a certain time in their lives; in other cases, it was more pervasive. Sometimes the distance seemed linked more to the father's character traits; other times it was more circumstantial. Also, the sons themselves may have projected their own distortions onto their fathers, contributing in their own ways to the distance between them. In all cases, the sons felt alienated from their fathers to some degree, at least at certain points in time. In comparison to this dynamic, the homosexuality seemed much less disturbing to them.

Elliot experienced his father as much less available during the period when Jonathon was coming out. Spending less time at home, his dad was obviously preoccupied with coming to terms with being gay and negotiating changes that would have far-reaching consequences for himself and his family. Thirteen-year-old Richard says he would like his dad to be a more active presence in his life now—to speak with him more, to initiate conversation more, and to let him know what he's thinking more of the time. Andy's father was physically absent for most of his son's life. Living in Florida, Miguel succumbed to AIDS when Andy was only seventeen.

Shawn's father was somewhat uneven in his involvement—less involved when his son was a youngster, a bit overinvolved once his son hit adolescence. Always the disciplinarian, his father became more demanding and rigid, particularly after he came out, partly to prove his competence as a (gay) parent—demanding perfect grades from Shawn and actively discouraging any form of self-expression which others might have construed as gay.

In contrast, Eric has *always* seen his father as detached, "remote," "secretive," hard to understand, and, as a result, hard to feel close to. Mark experiences his dad as emotionally inconsistent ("being there but not really being there"), defensive, hard to confront, and having a strong need to orchestrate situations and control others' reactions. In all fairness, he says that John has made some gains in these areas in recent years.

Thomas describes his father as self-centered—always needing to be in "the spotlight," frequently subordinating the needs of others to his own needs, and judging others swiftly and with "total confidence." Eric also uses the term *judgmental* about his dad, describing his father as "downright moralistic." Going even further, Noah perceives his dad as being bigoted (judging whole groups of people on the behavior of a few) and hypocritical at times (lying to Noah on occasion despite his protestations against lying and taking a stand against pornography but hiding pornographic magazines). Paul also thinks of his father as very much a hypocrite, a man privately homosexual but publicly heterosexual.

Then there were fathers who related to their sons in destructive ways, ways that caused rifts between them, sometimes for years. Joseph and his father had some physical confrontations during his adolescence, the result of his father's frustrations about being in a marriage he didn't believe in and being in a career that hadn't been especially successful.

On a whole different level is Paul's father, again in a class by himself, a man who sexually abused his son continuously for about twelve years. The chasm this abuse created between them took many years to mend and heal.

Some of the sons, such as Rob and Matthew, may have projected some of their own fears onto what their fathers were doing, contributing to the distance between them. After Warren came out, Rob became aware that his father had been dating men close to his son's age. Fears of abandonment emerged: was Rob going to be replaced by these other men?

Matthew's fears of abandonment went deeper and lasted longer. Even as a youngster, he felt his dad was on the brink of leaving him and their family. Being at home less and at work more, Matthew had practically convinced himself that his father was having an affair with another woman. These fears ebbed and flowed throughout much of his life.

Fathers and Sons Now

Asking the sons when the best times in their relationships with their fathers were, Richard, Joseph, Paul, Noah, Elliot, and Shawn, all either implied or explicitly stated that *now* was the best time. For Richard, the conflicts between his parents, so intolerable when they were all living together, are no longer an issue in the same ways because they are divorced and living in separate apartments. Both Joseph and Paul have worked through their anger at their fathers and have now reached a point of forgiveness for all the abuse and abandonment perpetrated earlier in their lives. Paul, Noah, Elliot, and Shawn all say that their relationships with their fathers have taken on the quality of a friendship. Man to man, they now feel more on equal footing.

Although Matthew also says that his dad seems more like a peer than ever before, that does not necessarily mean, for him, that now is their best time. Rather, he recalls moments of intimacy together, particularly in his early adolescence when father and son "bonded" on camping trips. Mark has had a similar experience. Trips taken as a family or just the two of them together, in the past and in the present, provided a perfect opportunity for a meeting of the minds and an emotional intimacy between father and son that have been difficult to achieve in other ways.

For Thomas, although the level of anger with his father has dissipated somewhat over the past few years, little real communication exists between them. Thomas attributes their disconnection more now to his dad than he used to. Before he was made to feel that it was entirely his fault. Now he realizes it takes "two to tango." Rob suggests that his relationship with his father has not fundamentally changed over the years. For Eric, the distance between himself and his father is greater than ever.

In addition, for Matthew and Rob, a period of reversal took place. Both assumed a quasiparental role—in effect becoming fathers to their fathers. After Matthew's dad came out, Dan would call his son and express his sadness about the separation from his wife and the frustrations of being newly single and beginning to date again. Matthew became father/mediator/therapist/advisor/friend to his father, all rolled into one. Similarly for Rob, he was upset about his father's impulsivity when meeting men online as well as his lapses in judgment in dating men his son's age. Rob became the father and Warren played the adolescent son, admonished for making poor "choices." Rob would also ask his father if he was using "protection."

In many cases, the sons see their fathers as happier, healthier people who are slowly, inevitably, moving toward a genuine sense of themselves, some farther along than others. Elliot feels a great deal of respect for his father "for doing what he did" and thinks "he's probably more himself now than he ever was." Although Rob was upset with his father for what he perceived as his poor judgment and impulsivity, he now says Warren is "starting to make some good choices in life. He's . . . getting there, slowly but surely." Mark had a tremendous amount of anger with his dad for being so defensive, so controlling, and so avoiding of the big emotional issues for so long. He thinks that John is now "working really hard at" being more open and available, and admires his father's bravery for coming out, knowing that "he could have gone the other way and just . . . disappeared." Joseph says his father is "happier now than he's ever been. He really likes his relationship and they've been together a long, long time. . . . He's found what he's needed in life, his calling." Richard reports that his father told him that "he's really happy." Noah's dad came out twice: first as a gay man, and second as a drag entertainer, thereby fulfilling two parts of himself. Matthew experiences his dad as being in a state of transition right now. He salutes him "for choosing to be honest with [him]self " and with those he loves and for "doing something very, very difficult." However, newly adjusting to single gay life has not been easy for Dan, but he is making gains.

Shawn has watched his father grow more and more comfortable with himself over time, though he thinks his dad was happier when he was involved in his long-term relationship. Now that he is romantically unattached and without a real group of friends, Shawn worries about him. Thomas doesn't experience his father as changed at all since he came out. Paul's father continues to remain closeted, despite the fact that the whole family is aware that he is gay. Even though his father is quite open with his son and his son's lover, they are the only ones he speaks to about this part of himself.

Eric and his father are at their lowest point ever. The growing schism is built on many complex factors stemming from both the past and present. His father's rather detached character style coupled with Eric's extreme discomfort about the ways his father and his lover continue to live their lives—bringing others in and out of their relationship in different ways—serve to distance the two from each other with increasing frequency. As Eric reminds us, "Not all of this is about sexual orientation. . . . This is about my father."

The different types of formal and informal support the sons sought after learning about their dads' homosexuality helped them deal more effectively with it. Matthew marched in the local Gay Pride parade, then joined COLAGE within the year after his father disclosed. This organization exposed him to a wider range of people than he had known and helped him come face to face with his own homophobia and redefine what the concept of *family* meant.

Shawn saw an educational videotape as a teenager called *Not All Parents Are Straight*. It was a relief to discover there were, in fact, other kids like him out there. Performing music has also been immeasurable in its power to soothe and heal, a way for him to come to terms with the more difficult things in his life. As an adult, Shawn tried to start a COLAGE chapter but failed to find enough people who expressed an interest. He also attended PFLAG, although he found the "vibe" too "Kumbaya." Elliot attended PFLAG too as a teenager but felt it to be a "forced" activity and not useful for him at the time. Richard, in contrast, sometimes attends PFLAG and Bear meetings with his father and finds those helpful. Noah attends his dad's drag performances as well as concerts and events connected with the Gay Men's Chorus.

Mark, Elliot, Rob, Matthew, Eric, Shawn, and Paul all underwent therapy, some of them to deal specifically with the ramifications of the disclosure and what it meant, others to deal with their lives as a whole. Elliot also sought the counsel of trusted adults he knew—a school guidance counselor and an adult friend.

Some turned to family, especially to their brothers and sisters. Although many, such as Eric, Rob, Mark, and Thomas, are close to their siblings, it was Elliot and Matthew especially who highlighted that relationship and the unique blend of support both offered and received, support that may not have been available from their mothers, who could have been mourning their own loss at the time.

Of interest was the fact that no participant cited any close friends his own age who specifically helped him through this experience. Although many disclosed to a selected, trusted few either before the disclosure (such as Noah) or after it, friends were among the last to know. Fear of ridicule, humiliation, and ostracism were present, even for adults such as Andy. To date, he has discussed his dad's homosexuality only with his wife, his aunt, and his uncle. He has never talked about it with his mother and has no plans to tell any of his friends now, possibly ever. He doesn't want to risk losing their respect or possibly their friendship entirely: "I'd be scared that they wouldn't look at me the same." Since his father was gay, they might think he is too.

When asking the sons if their father being gay has affected them, three of them report little specific impact on their lives. Rob says that "it hasn't really affected [him] any way different." Thomas considers it "a nonissue." Joseph thinks his father is his father regardless of sexual orientation. It is, however, something he is "proud" to tell his own gay friends.

In contrast, seven participants feel there have been positive changes for them since the disclosure. Thirteen-year-old Richard acknowledges all the new people he has met and all the different perspectives he has been exposed to. Elliot thought that his dad coming out led to many questions about his own beliefs, not only relative to sexuality but also to religion, marriage, and morality.

Around the time Matthew's father disclosed, Matthew was questioning his values and ideas about many things. Dan's disclosure proved yet another catalyst for change, presenting opportunities for learning about the wider world through his involvement with COLAGE. He also influenced his father to be more of an activist in gay political causes, a shift that Matthew feels very good about. It has also opened up all of the relationships in his family as never before. Likewise, Shawn now has a greater awareness "of the complexity of sexuality and humanity," a greater "tolerance for those who are different through no choice of their own," and a greater "willingness to stand up for those who are persecuted for the sake of righteousness."

For Mark, it has exposed him to a part of life he never would have had to confront in the same way and provided him with clarity about the many facets of family life that might have been shrouded in darkness forever. For Noah, his father's homosexuality has fostered an open-minded attitude and presented the opportunities of getting the best of all possible worlds—two sets of parents who love and cherish him. Although Andy feels that he has missed out on the chance to share his life with his father, who died in his prime, he thinks that Miguel, without either of them being aware of it, was influential in his cultivating a more androgynous persona—a combination of masculine and feminine qualities—which has immeasurably enriched Andy as a person.

For Eric, although the disclosure left him anxiety ridden for many years, it was just one factor that created the many obstacles he has had to face. Overcoming those obstacles has made him the person he is today and allowed him, in a professional capacity, to help other people overcome theirs.

Similarly with Paul, it was hard to know exactly when, but because of the sexual abuse—*not* because of his father's sexual orientation—he developed a type of dissociative disorder known as *depersonalization,* a state in which there is a sense of detachment from one's mental processes, as if one is in a dream. His psychic survival depended on actively separating himself from the abuse while it was taking place. On a deeper level, he remained confused for many years about his own sexual identity, not fully coming to terms with it until after his twelve-year marriage fell apart. He thought that any feelings he had for men were exclusively related to the abuse, not to being gay. Over time, Paul learned to confront his demons, making him a stronger, more confident person, now able to confront other challenges of life as never before.

Chapter 6

Discussion

Shades of the prison-house begin to close
Upon the growing Boy,
But He beholds the light, and whence it flows,
He sees it in his joy;

Wordsworth
"Intimations of Immortality
from Recollections of Early Childhood"

Our task now is to take all that has gone before this and place it into a context; to use what we have learned about the sons and conceptualize that understanding in a broader way. As I pointed out in Chapter 3, where you begin is not necessarily where you end. At the outset, I felt that I was trying to squeeze a square peg into a round hole. Although I started by exploring the son's experience of having a gay father, I ended up exploring the son's experience of having a father who happens to be gay. Sexuality was secondary. Other apects of their fathers mattered more to these sons in the final analysis. Gay or not gay, a father is *still* a father.

Qualitative research is an open-ended process. It questions rather than answers; it suggests rather than defines. Using some of my ideas from *Out of the Twilight* as points of departure and comparison, following are some other ideas that have come out of this study. I end with some research and clinical suggestions and a personal observation.

LEVELS OF ACCEPTANCE

In *Out of the Twilight,* I delineated three levels of acceptance of a family member's homosexuality: *resigned, narcissistic,* and *uncondi-*

tional. Of these, the first and last ones are applicable here. Andy and Rob typify an attitude of *resigned acceptance.* One of Andy's responses to finding out about his father was, "You know what? I love him anyway." Andy loved his dad *despite* his having been gay. Since he found out about his father's homosexuality only four months before the initial interview, he has had less time to process it than the rest of the sons have. This may be further complicated by the fact that his dad is no longer alive. Andy will neither discuss it with his friends because of his fear that they might feel less comfortable with him and reject him, nor with his mother because of his fear of upsetting her. Rob says of his father, "I kind of wished that he had stayed the way he was just 'cause that's how I knew him." Both Andy and Rob would, ideally, want things a different way but are doing their best to live with what they cannot change. They are resigned to the reality.

Unconditional acceptance is captured best by Thomas's words: "I accepted him as he was." Similar to Thomas, all of the sons, besides Andy and Rob, seem to accept their fathers unconditionally—as they are. Joseph says, "It's what he wanted to do and if he's happy, God bless him." Noah now more freely tells others about his entire family, which includes "dad and his husband," and keeps a picture of his father "as runner-up Miss New York" on his wall. He corrects those who think it's his mom by saying, "Actually, that's my dad!" Richard has always been "OK" with his father's homosexuality. Matthew marched during Gay Pride Day and joined COLAGE shortly after the disclosure. Elliot is "really happy it has all worked out this way in the end, knowing that it could never have been any different." Shawn watched as his father struggled for many years and acknowledges that "having a self-identity that you can live with is priceless." For Mark, his father's sexuality has never been the real issue. It was more about how his father controlled the information and controlled others with it.

Paul and Eric seem more accepting of their fathers than the fathers are of themselves. Paul's dad is still married and will probably stay married. Although very open with his son, Paul is "forced to keep his secret out of not wanting to hurt his wife." Eric wishes his "father were prouder of being gay" than he obviously is. Staunchly conservative, his dad supports people such as Rush Limbaugh and thinks "the military would fall apart" if gays were allowed in indiscriminately: "Give a queen an inch, he'll take a mile." Since most of the sons are unconditional in their acceptance, our task is to hypothesize about how they could have arrived at that point.

THE ADAPTIVE SON

As I explored the histories of the sons, I was struck by the many changes some of them had to contend with throughout their lives. Geographical shift was one of those changes. Moving to different locations, mostly to different cities or to a different living arrangement within the same area, occurred with some frequency. Those moves were mostly necessitated by their fathers' work or by the parents' separation, or were part of trying to create a better, more stable living situation for the entire family, or a combination of these.

In addition, all of the sons had to deal with their parents' separation and divorce. The reasons for the split were *not* understood by the sons as solely connected to the father's homosexuality. In two cases, the wives did not even know their husbands were gay until afterward; in the cases of Paul and Rob, *both* parents were gay and lesbian; and in some cases personality factors exacerbated the conflict between husband and wife. Whatever the reasons were for the separation, this event occurred at different points in the sons' lives—from infancy, as in Andy's case, through adulthood, as in Matthew's case.

Some had a more difficult time with it than others. For example, when five-year-old Noah's parents separated, his mother and his mother's boyfriend all moved to California together, which meant leaving his dad, a pretty difficult thing considering how close father and son were. Mark was seven when his parents separated. Their constant fighting was very disturbing for him, especially since he had no idea what it was about. Shawn, ten years old at the time, describes the separation as "bloody fucking awful," leaving him feeling totally powerless. His family, his "refuge . . . was blowing up for reasons" he could not comprehend. For Richard, who was around the same age as Shawn, the time before the separation was "brutal" and the worst period in his young life.

Things were equally brutal for Elliot and Joseph, thirteen and fifteen years old respectively, when their parents were splitting up. Elliot says that time was the lowest point in his life. Joseph recalls that all the conflict in his household came to a climax the day his father walked out, setting the stage for his own delinquent activity. Even for Matthew, an adult living independently when his father disclosed and when his parents began their formal separation, there are problems he now faces, such as whose house he is going to stay at when he goes for a visit and attempting to negotiate a role he is comfortable with in relation to each of his parents.

There were also corollary conflicts. Although Andy was an infant and Eric was about three years old when their parents separated, they eventually had to deal with difficult relationships with their stepfathers, some of whom had their own problems. Eric's stepfather was a gambler and an alcoholic. Andy describes his stepfather as "ignorant," always in competition with Andy, a man who never made an effort to befriend him. Shawn's problem with his stepfather, an all-around nice guy, was more about Shawn not wanting to accept discipline from someone who was not his father, which meant accepting another parent into his life, something he did not want. Matthew now struggles with accepting his mother's husband-to-be. In Elliot's situation, it was difficult accepting his father's new partner, a man he felt took no interest in him and whom, in turn, Elliot took no interest in.

Even though the majority of the mothers eventually had another partner in their lives or remarried, some of the sons may have felt the need to take care of their mothers and be "the man of the house" after their fathers left. Although being an *Oedipal victor*—a position in which the boy replaces his father in relation to the mother—stimulates a sense of being powerful, it can ultimately lead to a sense of being powerless. Deep down, boys—little boys *and* adolescent boys—know they are not really up to that task. Were the sons angry with their fathers for putting them in a position they did not feel psychologically prepared for?

Sometimes change also meant being part of an entirely new family configured in various ways: Andy's mother and stepfather had a daughter; Noah's mother and stepfather also had a daughter and his father's partner had a daughter from a previous marriage; Mark's father and stepmother had two children; Eric's mother and stepfather had three; Shawn's stepfather already had three from another marriage.

These changes were not equally difficult for all of them. Some fared better than others did. The degree to which these situations were about dislike of or discomfort with new parental figures and/or new stepsiblings or half siblings and how much of these situations were about the difficulties adjusting to a radical change in who constituted their families should be considered.

The question is: did experiencing all of these changes—the moves, the separations and divorces, the new stepparents, the new stepsiblings or half siblings—make the sons more adaptive, either preparing them for the disclosure to come or relegating the disclosure to a secondary issue? About his parents' separation and divorce Shawn says, "Dad coming out wasn't even remotely resembling traumatic after that stuff." Further, did having to adapt to these changes help the sons identify with the fathers in their own struggle to adapt to change? Would *identification*—that "perception of a common quality shared with some other person" (Freud, 1921/1971, p. 49)—or, as Bozett (1987a; 1988b) calls it, *mutuality,* make them more sensitive to and accepting of their fathers' homosexuality?

Devaluation

The fathers in *Out of the Twilight* tended to idealize their sons. They considered them special in different ways: physically attractive, exceptionally creative or artistic, highly intelligent, and in possession of superior character. In contrast, the sons in this study devalued their fathers in some ways, considered them detached, avoidant, rigid, controlling, hypocritical, prejudicial, danger seeking, impulsive, abusive, secretive, and narcissistic. These weaknesses in character were highlighted to the same extent that the homosexuality was minimized. Did *devaluation,* or a "depreciated view" (Goldstein, 1995, p. 83) of certain aspects of their fathers, serve as a defense against dealing with their homosexuality, just as *idealization* did for the fathers in *Twilight?* Was it how they really felt—that their fathers' sexuality did not matter as much as other limitations? Or was it a combination of the two?

In *Twilight,* I highlighted the final stage of life, a time when people especially need to see their lives as productive and worthwhile, and feel a sense that they have made a lasting contribution. Part of that contribution includes their children. If they feel their offspring have been successful, then they themselves feel successful. *Idealization* or overestimation becomes a major adaptive mechanism for a father to feel good about himself and good about his place in the world. If my son is special, then I, who have made him, am special, too. His narcissism becomes restored after sustaining whatever psychic injury he may have had by virtue of having a gay son.

However, unlike the father, who must relinquish power at the end of his life, the son, through his own assertion, must ultimately replace his father. It is partly through devaluation that this is accomplished. Through his aggression, he shrinks his father, making him become like the child he himself was years ago. Given this developmental reality, it might have seemed natural for the father's homosexuality to come under attack along with the other more negative character traits. Why didn't it?

I can discern four reasons. First, the other weaknesses of the fathers I highlighted previously are ones considered amenable to change. In contrast, sexual orientation does not change, perhaps making it easier for the sons to accept.

Second, the defense of *intellectualization,* or the act of thinking about feelings as opposed to experiencing them (Goldstein, 1995), was not uncommon. Rob illustrates this when he talks about that he would rather his father stay heterosexual since that was the way he knew him: "I understand that . . . he's got a life that he lives and . . . he's almost sixty now so, I mean, who am I to stop him from living how he wants to live?" He is employing reasoning to buffer feeling. Rob *understands* why his dad did what he had to, but had there been a choice Rob would rather it be different.

Third, to be confronted by a parent's homosexuality is to be confronted by the fact that the parent is *sexual,* and most children do not want to envision their parents in that way—gay or straight. Mark refers to this when he says, "I . . . don't really want to think about my dad in that kind of sexual way." To think about parents as sexual is to also have to think about them as *human*. Maybe that is the hard part. Would we like to retain a concept of our fathers as the idealized, omnipotent figures we knew from early childhood, the father who protected us, the father whom we loved passionately, the pre-Oedipal father (Blos, 1985)?

Fourth, and perhaps most important, it is my belief that their fathers' homosexuality represents the *true self,* the self that acts spontaneously, creatively, genuinely. At first fragile, vulnerable, protected, hidden by the *false self,* the self that is built around expectations of others, the true self, in contrast, grows into its own under the right conditions, over time (Winnicott, 1960/1965). Matthew likens this to a play, watching his dad step out of the character he showed the world and finally step into himself, thus making Matthew himself feel more "real" in the process. For the sons to attack the true self might be to psychically destroy the father completely—a radical step. Although developmentally a son needs to replace his father, he doesn't want him out of the way entirely. That would induce too much guilt and, ultimately, leave him fatherless. A son loves his father and he, in turn, needs to be loved *by* his father.

From Secrecy to Openness

A son wants to know who his father is. Whatever the answer, it is usually less disturbing than *not* knowing. Clearly the trait that made the sons feel most angry, frustrated, and helpless was their fathers' distance, which took many forms. One of those forms included silence about their sexuality. Revealing their sexuality seemed to be more of a risk for the fathers than a problem for the sons. The fears of a loss of power connected to being a member of a stigmatized group coupled with the threats of being abandoned by their families were probably at the core of their fathers' anxiety about disclosing. However, *not* disclosing was clearly more destructive, leaving the son to wonder, even obsess, about what was the problem was. A father's full presence in his son's life is what matters most. It is not who your father is or what he is. It is *that* he is.

Beeler and DiProva (1999) make reference to the concept of *restorying.* By this they mean the capacity to look back on our life history, reexamine it, and retell it in light of new information, thereby achieving *narrative coherency* (pp. 452-453). Several of the sons made reference to this phenomenon.

Thomas said that the knowledge of his father's homosexuality "explained so many things. Suddenly so many past images fit together." Finally he understood who the man was living at the top of their mansion, why his father dressed so idiosyncratically, and why there were no other women in his dad's life after his parents separated. Similarly,

Matthew says, "I just kept going back over my whole life and replaying it in this different context." For him it explained his dad's manner of dress, his sensitivity, and his difference from the other fathers he knew: "Over a period of months . . . I would process my whole life over again, putting my 'new' dad in where my 'old' dad was." It also shed light on why his family was so socially isolated over the years and why Matthew now has to struggle so hard to work against that tendency in himself. For Joseph, it helped him to "forgive" his father for leaving, knowing now that there had been "something else calling" him. For Mark, it not only explained much about his father's behaviors. It also helped him to explain his mother's behaviors, as well as to develop a greater empathy for both parents: "When you look back at memories from childhood with new understanding, how much it changes your understanding of those memories and almost changes the memory."

When I asked the sons why they wanted to participate in this study, I got a range of answers: to receive the gratification that comes from being in a book; to get the satisfaction of helping those who have found themselves in a similar circumstance; to gain exposure to others who have gone through this and compare oneself to them; to educate; to support their father; and to help themselves talk about this issue more openly than they might have otherwise. One of them even said that their desire to participate might be connected to some need to retaliate against the father through the act of exposure.

Secrets can be kept for a long time. After a point, however, they begin to eat away at the very fabric of the family and of the self. Some of the fathers had kept their secret for many years and may have unknowingly projected their own shame onto their families. The sons used their participation as a way to examine this whole experience, to help shed whatever negative feelings they might still have about it, as well as to talk about their relationship with their fathers apart from his sexuality. The fathers' secrecy stood in stark contrast to their sons' openness.

Also, for most of them, there was a sense of isolation they currently experience in not knowing others who have gay parents. Involvement in this study was, I think, some attempt to bridge that gap and facilitate their own coming out. The shared stigma or *courtesy stigma* (Goffman, 1986) of being gay and being the child of a gay parent also serves as another point of identification.

LIMITATIONS AND IMPLICATIONS
FOR FUTURE RESEARCH

As I observed earlier, this study, similar to other qualitative studies, is based on a small sample. Most of the sons had achieved unconditional acceptance of their fathers' homosexuality; it was no longer an issue. For some it had never been. What about those sons who cannot get beyond this fact of life? What are the impediments and how do those impact on their relationships with their fathers and with their families as a whole? This study does not pretend to represent the experience of all sons; only those who have been able to achieve some level of acceptance came forward and could be represented. We know that, typically, those who are rejecting of their gay family member do not tend to reveal themselves publicly. How to locate them is problematic. Their own shame keeps them in hiding.

Another limitation is that these sons, who are mostly middle class, well educated, and Caucasian, were all born in the context of a heterosexual marriage. They found out about their fathers' homosexuality *after* the fact. It was not a given. What about those sons who grow up with the full knowledge that their fathers are gay? Are they different from the sons in this study? What about those sons whose fathers adopt them? Does not being a blood relative matter one way or the other?

With the possible exceptions of Thomas and Mark, who both lived with their fathers full-time beginning in midadolescence, the majority of the sons spent roughly the same amount of time with both parents or more time with their mothers while growing up. What about sons who are raised predominately by their gay dads? What would they be like?

Another surprise that arose here, as was the case in *Twilight,* was that, except for Eric and Elliot, the disclosure, while usually creating a family crisis, did *not* create a crisis for the sons individually. What made it a crisis for the two of them? Although both were in their early adolescence, that fact alone is not enough to explain it. Thomas,

Richard, and Shawn were around that age. What other factors enter into the picture?

Who one is told *by* and their feelings about it also have an effect. Eric was informed first by his mother. Her shame and disgust were all too apparent, something Eric then internalized. Mark's mother hinted about his father's homosexuality rather than offering anything conclusive. Thomas, around the same age as both Eric and Mark when he found out, was also told by his mother, but she presented it more neutrally. Thomas's relief was unlike the responses of the other two. What are the effects of a disclosure made by someone else either directly or indirectly versus a direct, verbal disclosure confidently made by the gay person himself?

Does being gay shape one's individual parenting style? A continuum was definitely observed here. On one end was Matthew's father, who was always extremely physical with his son while growing up and very open about sexuality (except his own). In contrast was Shawn's father, never "much of a hands-on dad," who became even more rigid after his disclosure in order to prove his competence. He was also very concerned that others might think his son was gay, so he actively discouraged any form of Shawn's self-expression which might be so construed. Is how these fathers deal with being a gay parent a function of personality style, a function of their feelings about being gay, or a combination of these factors?

Do self-help groups such as COLAGE and PFLAG help? Not including the two gay sons in the study, some others, such as Matthew, Shawn, Richard, Elliot, and Noah, had either taken part in or are presently involved with some kind of group for gay people and their families. They were among the same sons who, I think, have the strongest relationships with their fathers. This was a conclusion I reached in *Twilight* as well. The fathers in that study who had attended PFLAG were those whom I considered to be closest to their sons. My guess is that participation in these groups seems to strengthen what is *already* a good relationship with the gay family member. Those more estranged would not typically seek that kind of support. It would be interesting, however, to study who joins these organizations, for what reasons, whether they feel helped and, if so, how.

Finally, in looking at the sons' responses to their fathers' homosexuality, one also has to factor in that we now live in a political climate that is, incrementally, more gay friendly. Societal change combined with personal change as young adults helped to move them toward full unconditional acceptance. Although these external variables are impossible to isolate and measure, they at least deserve mention.

IMPLICATIONS FOR CLINICAL PRACTICE

The goal of research is not only to expose us to types of situations that may not be accessible day to day, but to help us understand those situations and know how to more effectively intervene when we do encounter them. Although qualitative research and clinical practice are different in fundamental ways, they are also the same in other ways. To engage, to explore, and to understand are common to both disciplines. The stance a qualitative researcher takes is the same one a clinician must take: assume nothing. Be aware of your bias and keep it aside. Whatever you have heard others say about this situation is useful as a backdrop, but it may not tell you much about the person sitting before you. Let the story unfold as naturally as you can. Your job is to help them tell it.

Other recommendations for practice are clear. Those initiating treatment precipitated by the disclosure might be quite confused about what this means for their relationships with their gay parent, with the rest of their families, and particularly with their friends. At the bottom of whatever feelings they may have about it—anger, shock, surprise, fear, confusion, embarrassment, shame—invariably lies a sense of loss. What that loss is exactly you will have to uncover. As I pointed out in Chapter 2 and as we have seen in the stories, loss can take many forms: a loss of trust in a parent they thought they knew; the loss of a heterosexual role model; the loss of stability during and after of the breakup of their family; the loss of an earlier role they had and the uncertainty about taking on a new one; a loss of status in their family and in their community; a loss of a parent from AIDS; a loss of certainty about one's own identity; a loss in the belief that anything in the world is safe and predictable. Whatever the case, you must help them clarify and mourn those losses. Further, you must also be alert as to whether the homosexuality is the real issue or if it is just a smoke screen for other unresolved conflicts that have lain dormant and are now being activated by the disclosure.

After that, the clinical task becomes one of helping to build a sense of identification with the gay parent. Are they similar to them or different from them? Many of the sons told me how much alike they thought they were to their fathers in relation to their interests, their intellect, their physical appearance, and their temperaments. Slowly, over time, use that as one way to reestablish the connection if one has been broken. Helping them to see similarity while learning respect for difference is key. Converting danger into opportunity becomes the central task of treatment.

EPILOGUE

Patterson (1992) delineates three areas of concern frequently raised about children of gay parents: (1) their sexual identity will be confused or they themselves will be gay; (2) they will be emotionally less stable; and (3) their social development will be negatively affected. Underneath these concerns is the fear that these children will not be the same as others raised in more traditional households, as if being the same is always such a positive thing. There is also the assumption here that a gay parent is, as I discussed in the Introduction, a contradiction in terms, that their influence could only be an adverse one. The belief seems to be that not only would gay parents create turmoil in their children, they would not be able to help the children face any of the negative repercussions, if any, that occurred outside the home. It also assumes that children are not resilient. Society seems to see only the danger as opposed to the opportunity.

You have read the stories of these sons. You can judge for yourself how successful or unsuccessful their development has been over time. Two of the twelve sons turned out to be gay. All are either in school or engaged in meaningful work. Many of them are in committed, intimate relationships. Paul's story is an unfortunate one in some ways. The sexual abuse he suffered had a traumatizing effect on him. He has had to fight long and hard to recover from it. Yet recover he has: now he is stronger than ever, despite and because of his past.

It would be nice if we lived in a world in which writing a book such as this was unnecessary—a world in which fathers wouldn't have to hide who they are, in which children wouldn't be forced to hold secrets, in which a gay parent wouldn't be considered a contradiction in terms.

As much as I would like to believe that this could happen, I realize it probably won't any time soon. Maybe we can inch toward it, but there will probably always be some parents who will try to conceal who they are from their children and from themselves. Families pay dearly for that secrecy in relationships that are diminished in feeling and in experience.

In this study, I have taken the long view, seeing the disclosure not as a separate act but rather in the context of a relationship where it belongs. Coming out as gay does not usually make or break that relationship. It is only one moment in a sequence of moments. One must look at what took place before it and what takes place after it in order to understand its meaning and its impact. Families can survive if there is a solid foundation to begin with. If no solid base exists, it presents yet another opportunity—a second chance—to build one together.

Appendix A

Consent Form

If you sign below, you are choosing to participate in this research project exploring the experiences of sons who have learned of their fathers' homosexuality. Your participation is voluntary. You may choose to withdraw at any time without any penalty or repercussions.

There will be one or two audiotaped interviews conducted solely by myself, lasting in duration from one to two hours each, or an in-person interview and follow-ups done by e-mail, or an interview and follow-ups exclusively done by e-mail. The tapes/transcripts will be given a number known only to me and may be reviewed by you. I will honor your request that any or all of the contents be destroyed should you have reservations or be dissatisfied in any way. I will also request other kinds of materials that you may have in your possession—letters, diaries, for example—which might add another dimension to what you tell me. If you have any of these, allowing me access would be at your discretion. Your name and other identifying information will be altered in the write-up. No monetary compensation will be offered, but you will be given the research study itself, which will be published in book form by The Haworth Press.

Your willingness to talk about your experiences may be important to others. However, this process may be emotionally difficult for you. Should any discomfort arise or you feel a need to continue talking about issues that are raised, I will discuss this with you further and a referral for counseling may be offered and arranged with your full consent.

If you have any further questions before, during, or after you have completed your participation, you may call me at _____, or write to me at _____, or e-mail me at _____.

Thank you very much for your interest.

_____   _____
Participant   Investigator

_____   _____
Date   Date

Appendix B

Semistructured Interview Guide

Would you tell me about your background—where did you grow up, who is in your family? How would you describe your father—what sort of a person he is, what things do you feel are important to him? What is your first memory of him? Describe your relationship with your father in the early years of your life. Are there any particular events that stand out? Describe your relationship with him through the present. What were the best times; the worst times? Has your relationship with him been the same or different than the one(s) he has with your sibling(s)? What are the similarities and difference between the two of you?

Did you ever think that he might be gay? If so, when was that and what was that like for you? When did you actually find out about his homosexuality? Was it a gradual awakening, or were you informed and by whom? What was your immediate response? How did you handle it? How was the disclo sure dealt with in terms of family and friends? What was the quality of your relationship like at that point? Do you deal with it differently now? Did your relationship change after the knowledge of his sexuality and, if so, how?

Did his homosexuality affect your feelings about yourself in any way? Did it affect your development in any way? Do you think there are any advantages and/or disadvantages to having a gay father? Has having a gay father affected you at all?

Appendix C

The Sons at a Glance

Mark, thirty-three, Sicilian/Welsh/Irish/French, born Catholic but nonpracticing, heterosexual, married, computer software developer: "Maybe just really big things have to happen to change your whole perspective."

Andy, twenty-seven, Cuban, Catholic, heterosexual, married, social worker: "I wish he was here. I wish he was still alive."

Noah, twenty-three, Canadian, Jewish/Catholic, heterosexual, single, medical student: "My life has been more a model of how . . . things can go right."

Joseph, forty-two, Austrian/Russian/Polish, Jewish, homosexual, single, interior artist: "He really does love me very much. And I love my dad."

Richard, thirteen, Norwegian/Irish/English/Cherokee, United Church of Christ, sexuality undetermined, junior high school student: "I'm there for him."

Shawn, thirty-one, Scottish/Irish/Welsh/English/German/Cherokee, Episcopalian, heterosexual, engaged, office manager/musician: "Our relationship now is as good as it has ever been."

Rob, twenty-one, English/German/Scottish/Swiss, Catholic but nonpracticing, heterosexual, single, college junior: "Life goes on."

Eric, forty-four, Swedish/English, Protestant, heterosexual, married, social worker: "There's always an effort to find . . . pieces of my father."

Paul III, forty-three, Scottish/Irish, Catholic, homosexual, partnered, manager for a large automobile corporation: "I can never forget . . . but I can forgive."

Elliot, twenty-six, German/English, raised Presbyterian but nonpracticing, heterosexual, single, graduate student: "He's probably more himself now than he ever was."

Thomas, twenty-two, Czech/Austro-Hungarian/German, born Jewish but non-practicing, heterosexual, single, works for a trading firm: "I accepted him as he was."

Matthew, twenty-seven, German/English/Norwegian/French/American Indian, Quaker/Protestant, heterosexual, single, computer software engineer: "I'm proud of *you* now."

References

Abelin, E. L. (1971). The role of the father in the separation-individuation process. In J. B. McDevitt and C. F. Settlage (Eds.), *Separation-individuation: Essays in honor of Margaret S. Mahler* (pp. 229-252). New York: International Universities Press.

_____ (1975). Some further observations and comments on the earliest role of the father. *International Journal of Psychoanalysis, 56,* 293-302.

Aleck, J. and Keily, J. (Producers) and MacKenzie, P. C. (Director) (2000). *Normal, Ohio* [Television Series]. The Carsey-Werner Company LLC, Fox Television Network.

Allen, D. (2002). The adoption option. *The Advocate,* May 28, 42-50.

Anderson, D. (1987). Family and peer relations of gay adolescents. *Adolescent Psychiatry: Developmental and Clinical Studies, 14,* 162-178.

Anderson, S. (1969). *Memoirs: A critical edition.* R. L. White (Ed.). Chapel Hill: The University of North Carolina Press.

Bailey, J. M., Bobrow, D., Wolfe, M., Mikach, S. (1995) Sexual orientation of adult sons of gay fathers. *Developmental Psychology, 31*(1), 124-129.

Baker, J. M. (1998). *Family secrets: Gay sons—A mother's story.* Binghamton, NY: Harrington Park Press.

_____ (2002). *How homophobia hurts children: Nurturing diversity at home, at school, and in the community.* Binghamton, NY: Harrington Park Press.

Barret, R. L. and Robinson, B. E. (1994). Gay dads. In A. E. Gottfried and A. W. Gottfried (Eds.), *Redefining families: Implications for children's development* (pp. 157-170). New York: Plenum Press.

_____ (2000). *Gay fathers: Encouraging the hearts of gay dads and their families* (New and revised edition). San Francisco, CA: Jossey-Bass.

Baum, M. I. (1996). Gays and lesbians choosing to be parents. In C. J. Alexander (Ed.), *Gay and lesbian mental health: A sourcebook for practitioners* (pp. 115-126). Binghamton, NY: Harrington Park Press.

Beeler, J. and DiProva, V. (1999). Family adjustment following disclosure of homosexuality by a member: Themes discerned in narrative accounts. *Journal of Marital and Family Therapy, 25*(4), 443-459.

Benjamin, J. (1995). *Like subjects, love objects: Essays on recognition and sexual difference.* New Haven, CT: Yale University Press.

Benkov, L. (1994). *Reinventing the family: Lesbian and gay parents.* New York: Crown Trade Paperbacks.

Bettelheim, B. (1977). *The uses of enchantment: The meaning and importance of fairy tales.* New York: Vintage Books.

Bigner, J. J. (1999). Raising our sons: Gay men as fathers. In T. R. Sullivan (Ed.), *Queer families, common agendas: Gay people, lesbians, and family values* (pp. 61-77). Binghamton, NY: Harrington Park Press.

Bigner, J. J. and Bozett, F. W. (1989). Parenting by gay fathers. *Marriage and Family Review, 14*(3/4), 155-175.

Bigner, J. J. and Jacobsen, R. B. (1989a). Parenting behaviors of homosexual and heterosexual fathers. *Journal of Homosexuality, 18*(1/2), 173-186.

_____ (1989b). The value of children to gay and heterosexual fathers. *Journal of Homosexuality, 18*(1/2), 163-172.

Bilsing, S., Buckner, B., Jones, S., Knoller, W., and Plummer, E. (Producers) and Bright, K. S. and Halvorson, G. (Directors) (2001). *Friends* [Television series]. NBC.

Blos, P. (1967). The second individuation process of adolescence. *The Psychoanalytic Study of the Child, 22,* 162-186.

_____ (1970). *The young adolescent: Clinical studies.* New York: The Free Press.

_____ (1985). *Son and father: Before and beyond the Oedipus complex.* New York: The Free Press.

Blumenfeld, W. J. (Ed.) (1992). *Homophobia: How we all pay the price.* Boston: Beacon Press.

Borhek, M. V. (1979). *My son Eric.* Cleveland, OH: The Pilgrim Press.

_____ (1993). *Coming out to parents: A two-way survival guide for lesbians and gay men and their parents* (Revised and updated edition). Cleveland, OH: The Pilgrim Press.

Bornstein, B. (1951). On latency. *The Psychoanalytic Study of the Child, 6,* 279-285.

Bozett, F. W. (1980). Gay fathers: How and why they disclose their homosexuality to their children. *Family Relations, 29*(2), 173-179.

_____ (1984). Parenting concerns of gay fathers. *Topics in Clinical Nursing, 6,* 60-71.

_____ (1985). Gay men as fathers. In S. M. H. Hanson and F. W. Bozett (Eds.), *Dimensions of fatherhood* (pp. 327-352). Beverly Hills, CA: Sage Publications.

_____ (1987a). Children of gay fathers. In F. W. Bozett (Ed.), *Gay and lesbian parents* (pp. 39-57). New York: Praeger.

_____ (1987b). Gay fathers. In F. W. Bozett (Ed.), *Gay and lesbian parents* (pp. 3-22). New York: Praeger.

_____ (1988a). Gay fatherhood. In P. Bronstein and C. P. Cowan (Eds.), *Fatherhood today: Men's changing role in the family* (pp. 214-235). New York: John C. Wiley and Sons.

_____ (1988b). Social control of identity by children of gay fathers. *Western Journal of Nursing Research, 10*(5), 550-565.

_____ (1989). Gay fathers: A review of the literature. *Journal of Homosexuality,* *18*(1/2), 137-162.

_____ (1990). Fathers who are gay. In R. J. Kus (Ed.), *Keys to caring: Assisting your gay and lesbian clients* (pp. 106-118). Boston: Alyson Publications, Inc.

Brager, E. A. (1989). G-strings for Daddy. In L. MacPike (Ed.), *There's something I've been meaning to tell you* (pp. 67-70). Tallahassee, FL: The Naiad Press, Inc.

Brammeier, S. (1989). Our trip to Chicago. In L. MacPike (Ed.), *There's something I've been meaning to tell you* (38-48). Tallahassee, FL: The Naiad Press, Inc.

Brill, S. A. (2001). *The queer parent's primer: A lesbian and gay families' guide to navigating the straight world.* Oakland, CA: New Harbinger Publications, Inc.

Buckner, R. (Producer) and Curtiz, M. (Director) (1981). *Life with father* [Film]. Los Angeles, CA: Media Home Entertainment, Inc.

Buxton, A. P. (1994). *The other side of the closet: The coming-out crisis for straight spouses and families* (Revised and expanded edition). New York: John Wiley and Sons, Inc.

_____ (1999). The best interest of children of gay and lesbian parents. In R. Galatzer-Levy and L. Kraus (Eds.), *The scientific basis of child custody decisions* (pp. 319-356). New York: John Wiley and Sons, Inc.

Clark, D. (1978*). Loving someone gay.* New York: New American Library.

_____ (1979). *Living gay.* Millbrae, CA: Celestial Arts.

Clermont, N. and King, P. (Producers) and Quinn, P. (Director) (1999). *This is my father* [Film]. Culver City, CA: Columbia TriStar Home Video.

Cohen, B. and Jinks, D. (Producers) and Mendes, S. (Director) (2000). *American Beauty* [Film]. Universal City, CA: Dreamworks Home Entertainment.

Cohn, A. and de Clermont-Tonnerre, M. (Producers) and Salles, W. (Director) (1999). *Central station* [Film]. Culver City, CA: Columbia TriStar Home Video.

Colarusso, C. A. and Nemiroff, R. A. (1981). The father at midlife: Crisis and growth of paternal identity. In C. A. Colarusso and R. A. Nemiroff (Eds.), *Adult development: A new dimension in psychodynamic theory and practice* (pp. 129-139). New York: Plenum Press.

Connelly, F. M. and Clandinin, D. J. (1990). Stories of experience and narrative inquiry. *Educational Researcher, 19*(5), 2-14.

Corley, R. (1990). *The final closet: The gay parents' guide for coming out to their children* (Revised edition). Miami, FL: Editech Press.

Cramer, D. (1986). Gay parents and their children: A review of research and practical implications. *Journal of Counseling and Development, 64,* 504-507.

De Milly III, W. A. (1999). *In my father's arms: A true story of incest.* Madison, WI: The University of Wisconsin Press.

Deevey, S. (1989). When mom or dad comes out: Helping adolescents cope with homophobia. *Journal of Psychosocial Nursing and Mental Health, 27*(10), 33-36.

DeVine, J. L. (1984). A systemic inspection of affectional preference orientation and the family of origin. *Journal of Social Work and Human Sexuality, 2*(2/3), 9-17.

Dew, R. F. (1995). *The family heart: A memoir of when our son came out.* New York: Ballatine Books.

Drucker, J. (1998). *Families of value: Gay and lesbian parents and their children speak out.* New York: Plenum Press.

Dunne, E. J. (1987). Helping gay fathers come out to their children. *Journal of Homosexuality, 14*(1/2), 213-222.

Ely, M., Anzul, M., Friedman, T., Garner, D., and Steinmetz, A. M. (1991). *Doing qualitative research: Circles within circles.* New York: The Falmer Press.

Esman, A. H. (1982). Fathers and adolescent sons. In S. H. Cath, A. R. Gurwitt, and J. M. Ross (Eds.), *Father and child: Developmental and clinical perspectives* (pp. 265-273). Boston: Little, Brown and Company.

Flotho, F. (1989). Coming out to Brian. In L. MacPike (Ed.), *There's something I've been meaning to tell you* (pp. 59-62). Tallahassee, FL: The Naiad Press, Inc.

Freud, A. (1966). *The writings of Anna Freud.* Volume II: *The ego and the mechanisms of defense* (Revised edition). New York: International Universities Press, Inc.

Freud, S. (1909/1977). Analysis of a phobia in a five-year-old boy. In A. Richards (Ed.), A. Strachey and J. Strachey (Trans.), *Case Histories I* (pp. 165-305). New York: Penguin Books.

_____ (1916-1917/1977). *Introductory lectures on psychoanalysis.* J. Strachey (Ed. and Trans.). New York: W. W. Norton and Company.

_____ (1918/1959). From the history of an infantile neurosis. In A. Strachey and J. Strachey (Trans.), *Collected papers* (Volume 3, pp. 471-605). New York: Basic Books, Inc.

_____ (1921/1971). *Group psychology and the analysis of the ego.* J. Strachey (Ed. and Trans.). New York: Bantam Books.

_____ (1923/1962). *The ego and the id.* J. Strachey (Ed.), J. Riviere (Trans.). New York: W. W. Norton and Company.

_____ (1925/1959). Some psychological consequences of the anatomical distinction between the sexes. In J. Strachey (Ed.), *Collected papers* (Volume 5, pp. 186-197). New York: Basic Books, Inc.

_____ (1927/1961). *The future of an illusion.* J. Strachey (Ed. and Trans.). New York: W. W. Norton and Company.

_____ (1933/1965). *New introductory lectures on psychoanalysis.* J. Strachey (Ed. and Trans.). New York: W. W. Norton and Company.

Gallagher, J. (1995). Gay . . . with children. *The Advocate,* May 30, 28-33.

Galluccio, J., Galluccio, M., and Groff, D. (2001). *An American family.* New York: St. Martin's Press.

Gantz, J. (1983). *Whose child cries: Children of gay parents talk about their lives.* Rolling Hill Estates, CA: Jalmar Press.

Garner, A. (1992). *Jack and the beanstalk.* New York: Delacourte Press.

Gierach, R. (2000-2001). Gayby Boom. *Genre,* December/January, 72-74.

Gochros, J. S. (1989). *When husbands come out of the closet.* Binghamton, NY: Harrington Park Press.

Goethe, J. W. (1786/1957). Erlkönig. In L. Forster (Ed.), *The Penguin Book of German Verse* (pp. 214-215). Baltimore, MD: Penguin Books.

Goffman, E. (1986). *Stigma: Notes on the management of spoiled identity* (First Touchstone edition). New York: Simon and Schuster, Inc.

Goldstein, E.G. (1995). *Ego psychology and social work practice* (Second edition). New York: The Free Press.

Golombok, S., Spencer, A., and Rutter, M. (1983). Children in lesbian and single-parent households: Psychosexual and psychiatric appraisals. *Journal of Child Psychology and Psychiatry, 24*(4), 551-572.

Gottlieb, A. R. (2000). *Out of the twilight: Fathers of gay men speak.* Binghamton, NY: Harrington Park Press.

Gottman, J. S. (1989). Children of gay and lesbian parents. *Marriage and Family Review, 14*(3/4), 177-196.

Green, J. (1999). *The velveteen father: An unexpected journey to parenthood.* New York: Ballantine Books.

Green, R. (1978). Sexual identity of 37 children raised by homosexual or transsexual parents. *The American Journal of Psychiatry, 135*(6), 692-697.

Green, R., Mandel, J. B., Hotvedt, M. E., Gray, J., and Smith, L. (1986). Lesbian mothers and their children: A comparison with solo parent heterosexual mothers and their children. *Archives of Sexual Behavior, 15*(2), 167-184.

Griffin, C. W., Wirth, M. J., and Wirth, A. G. (1986). *Beyond acceptance: Parents of lesbians and gays talk about their experiences.* Englewood Cliffs, NJ: Prentice-Hall, Inc.

Handel, L. (2000). *Now that you're out of the closet, what about the rest of the house?* Naperville, IL: Sourcebooks, Inc.

Harris, M. B. and Turner, P. H. (1986). Gay and lesbian parents. *Journal of Homosexuality, 12*(2), 101-113.

Herdt, G. and Koff, B. (2000). *Something to tell you: The road families travel when a child is gay.* New York: Columbia University Press.

Heron, A. and Maran, M. (1994). *How would you feel if your dad was gay?* Boston: Alyson Wonderland.

Herzog, J. M. (1980). Sleep disturbance and father hunger in 18- to 28-month-old boys: The erlkönig syndrome. *The Psychoanalytic Study of the Child, 35,* 219-233.

_____ (1982). On father hunger: The father's role in the modulation of aggressive drive and fantasy. In S. H. Cath, A. R. Gurwitt, and J. M. Ross (Eds.), *Father and child: Developmental and clinical perspectives* (pp. 163-174). Boston: Little, Brown and Company.

Hoeffer, B. (1981). Children's acquisition of sex-role behavior in lesbian-mother families. *American Journal of Orthopsychiatry, 51*(3), 536-544.

Homer (1963). *The odyssey.* Robert Fitzgerald (Trans.). New York: Anchor Books.

Homes, A. M. (1990). *Jack.* New York: Vintage Books.

Howey, N. and Samuels, E. (Eds.) (2000). *Out of the ordinary: Essays on growing up with gay, lesbian, and transgender parents.* New York: St. Martin's Press.

Huggins, S. L. (1989). A comparative study of self-esteem of adolescent children of divorced lesbian mothers and divorced heterosexual mothers. *Journal of Homosexuality, 18*(1/2), 123-135.

Jönsson, R. (1991). *My father, his son.* M. Ruuth (Trans.). New York: Arcade Publishing, Inc.

Joyce, J. (1916/1976). *A portrait of the artist as a young man.* New York: Penguin Books.

Kafka, F. (1919/1966). *Letter to his father.* E. Kaiser and E. Wilkins (Trans.). New York: Schocken Books.

Karslake, D. (Producer) (1999). Parenting comes out. On *In the life* [Television news magazine]. In the Life Media, Inc./PBS.

Kaufman, G. and Raphael, L. (1996). *Coming out of shame: Transforming gay and lesbian lives.* New York: Doubleday.

Kirkpatrick, M., Smith, C., and Roy, R. (1981). Lesbian mothers and their children: A comparative survey. *American Journal of Orthopsychiatry, 51*(3), 545-551.

Klein, F. and Schwartz, T. (Eds.). (2001). *Bisexual and gay husbands: Their stories, their words.* Binghamton, NY: Harrington Park Press.

Kweskin, S. L. and Cook, A. S. (1982). Heterosexual and homosexual mothers' self-described sex-role behavior and ideal sex-role behavior in children. *Sex Roles, 8*(9), 967-975.

Leavitt, D. (1987). *The lost language of cranes.* New York: Bantam Books.

Levinson, R. and Link, W. (Producers) and Johnson, L. (Director) (1972). *That certain summer* [Film]. ABC.

Lewis, K. G. (1980). Children of lesbians: Their point of view. *Social Work, 25*(3), 198-203.

Lynch, S. (2000). I remember reaching for Michael's hand. In N. Howey and E. Samuels (Eds.), *Out of the ordinary: Essays on growing up with gay, lesbian, and transgender parents* (pp. 63-71). New York: St. Martin's Press.

Mager, D. (1977). Faggot father. In K. Jay and A. Young (Eds.), *After you're out* (pp. 128-134). New York: Pyramid Books.

Mahler, M. S. and Gosliner, B. J. (1955). On symbiotic child psychosis: Genetic, dynamic and restitutive aspects. *The Psychoanalytic Study of the Child, 10,* 195-212.

Mahler, M. S., Pine, F., and Bergman, A. (1975). *The psychological birth of the human infant: Symbiosis and individuation.* New York: Basic Books, Inc.

Martin, A. (1993). *The lesbian and gay parenting handbook: Creating and raising our families.* New York: HarperPerennial.

Matousek, M. (2000). *The boy he left behind: A man's search for his lost father.* New York: Riverhead Books.

McCandlish, B. M. (1987). Against all odds: Lesbian mother family dynamics. In F. W. Bozett (Ed.), *Gay and lesbian parents* (pp. 23-36). New York: Praeger.

Miller, A. (1947/2000). *All my sons*. New York: Penguin.

_____ (1958). *Death of a salesman*. New York: Compass Books.

Miller, B. (1979). Gay fathers and their children. *The Family Coordinator, 28*(4), 544-552.

Miller, D. A. (1993). *Coping when a parent is gay*. New York: The Rosen Publishing Group, Inc.

Miller, J. A., Jacobsen, R. B., and Bigner, J. J. (1981). The child's home environment for lesbian vs. heterosexual mothers: A neglected area of research. *Journal of Homosexuality, 7*(1), 49-56.

Mirvis, P. H. and Louis, M. R. (1985). Self-full research: Working through the self as instrument in organizational research. In D. N. Berg and K. K. Smith (Eds.), *Exploring clinical methods for social research* (pp. 229-246). Beverly Hills, CA: Sage Publications.

Mishler, E. G. (1986). The analysis of interview-narratives. In T. R. Sarbin (Ed.), *Narrative psychology: The storied nature of human conduct* (pp. 233-255). New York: Praeger Special Studies.

Morgen, K. B. (1995). *Getting Simon: Two gay doctors' journey to fatherhood*. New York: Bramble Books.

Mucklow, B. M. and Phelan, G. K. (1979). Lesbian and traditional mothers' responses to adult response to child behavior and self-concept. *Psychological Reports, 44*, 880-882.

Neuberg, S. L., Smith, D. M., Hoffman, J. C., and Russell, F. J. (1994). When we observe stigmatized and "normal" individuals interacting: Stigma by association. *Personality and Social Psychology Bulletin, 20*(2), 196-209.

Nungesser, L. G. (1980). Theoretical bases for research on the acquisition of social sex-roles by children of lesbian mothers. *Journal of Homosexuality, 5*(3), 177-187.

Padgett, D. K. (1998). Does the glove really fit? Qualitative research and clinical social work practice. *Social Work, 43*(4), 373-381.

Pagelow, M. D. (1980). Heterosexual and lesbian single mothers: A comparison of problems, coping, and solutions. *Journal of Homosexuality, 5*(3), 189-204.

Parad, H. J. and Caplan, G. (1965). A framework for studying families in crisis. In H. J. Parad (Ed.), *Crisis intervention: Selected readings* (pp. 53-72). New York: Family Service Association of America.

Patterson, C. J. (1992). Children of lesbian and gay parents. *Child Development, 63*, 1025-1042.

Patterson, C. J. and Chan, R. W. (1996). Gay fathers. In M. E. Lamb (Ed.), *The role of the father in child development* (Third edition) (pp. 245-260). New York: John Wiley and Sons, Inc.

Pifer, A. I. (Producer) (2001). "The children speak." On *20/20* [Television series]. ABC.

Pine, F. (1989). The place of object loss in normal development. In D. R. Dietrich and P. C. Shabad (Eds.), *The problem of loss and mourning: Psychoanalytic perspectives* (pp. 159-173). Madison, CT: International Universities Press, Inc.

Pollack, J. S. (1995). *Lesbian and gay families: Redefining parenting in America.* New York: Franklin Watts.

Prall, R. C. (Reporter) (1978). The role of the father in the preoedipal years. *Journal of the American Psychoanalytic Association, 26,* 143-161.

Pratt, C. A. (Producer) and Carlino, L. J. (Director) (1981). *The great Santini* [Film]. Scarborough, Ontario: Orion Pictures/WEA Video.

Rand, C., Graham, D. L. R., and Rawlings, E. I. (1982). Psychological health and factors the court seeks to control in lesbian mother custody trials. *Journal of Homosexuality, 8*(1), 27-39.

Rapoport, L. (1965). The state of crisis: Some theoretical considerations. In H. J. Parad (Ed.), *Crisis intervention: Selected readings* (pp. 22-31). New York: Family Service Association of America.

Rawlings, M. K. (1938/1967). *The yearling.* New York: Aladdin Paperbacks.

Reid, W. J. and Smith, A. D. (1989). *Research in social work* (Second edition). New York: Columbia University Press.

Riddle, D. I. and Arguelles, M. d. L. (1981). Children of gay parents: Homophobia's victims. In I. R. Stuart and L. E. Abt (Eds.), *Children of separation and divorce: Management and treatment* (pp. 174-197). New York: Van Nostrand Reinhold Company.

Rorem, N. (1978). *An absolute gift.* New York: Simon and Schuster.

Rosenberg, T., Dixon, L., and Radmin, L. (Producers) and Schlesinger, J. (Director) (2000). *The next best thing* [Film]. Hollywood, CA: Lakeshore Entertainment Corporation and Paramount Pictures.

Roshan, M. (2000). Parenting: My two dads. *New York Magazine,* June 12, 48-52.

Ross, J. M. (1982). Oedipus revisited: Laius and the "Laius complex." *The Psychoanalytic Study of the Child, 37,* 169-200.

Rothstein, F. (Producer) and Brown, A. (Director) (1998). *Change of heart* [Film]. Tucson, AZ: Hearst Entertainment, Inc.

Saffron, L. (1996). Josh. In *What about the children?: Sons and daughters of lesbian and gay parents talk about their lives* (pp. 24-30). London: Cassell.

_____ (2001). *It's a family affair: The complete lesbian parenting book.* London: Diva Books.

Samuelson, M. and Samuelson, P. (Producers) and Gilbert, B. (Director) (1998). *Wilde* [Film]. Culver City, CA: Columbia TriStar Home Video.

Sartre, J. P. (1964). *The words.* B. Frechtman (Trans.). New York: George Braziller.

Savage. D. (1999). *The kid (What happened after my boyfriend and I decided to go get pregnant): An adoption story.* New York: Dutton.

Schulenburg, J. A. (1985). *Gay parenting: A complete guide for gay men and lesbians with children.* Garden City, NY: Anchor Press.

Shakespeare, W. (1988). *Hamlet.* D. Bevington (Ed.). New York: Bantam Books.

Shannon, G. (1995). *Unlived affections.* Los Angeles: Alyson Publications.

Sheehy, G. (1998). *Understanding men's passages: Discovering the new map of men's lives.* New York: Random House.

Siegel, S. and Lowe, E. Jr. (1995). *Uncharted lives: Understanding the life passages of gay men.* New York: Plume.

Slater, S. (1995). *The lesbian family life cycle.* New York: The Free Press.

Sophocles (1959). *Oedipus the king.* B. M. W. Knox (Trans.). New York: Washington Square Press, Inc.

Spadola. M. (Producer and Director) (1999). *Our house* [Documentary]. Sugar Pictures LLC, Independent Television Service.

Spradley, J. P. (1979). *The ethnographic interview.* New York: Holt, Rinehart and Winston.

Stern, D. N. (1990). *Diary of a baby.* New York: Basic Books, Inc.

Strauss, A. L. (1987). *Qualitative analysis for social scientists.* New York: Cambridge University Press.

Strommen, E. F. (1989). Hidden branches and growing pains: Homosexuality and the family tree. *Marriage and Family Review, 14*(3/4), 9-34.

Symons, J. (2001). Family matters. On *In the life* [Television news magazine]. In the Life Media, Inc./PBS.

Taylor, S. J. and Bogdan, R. (1984*). Introduction to qualitative research methods: The search for meanings* (Second edition). New York: John Wiley and Sons.

Thrasher, B. P. (1992). *Pinocchio.* London: Twin Books.

Tyson, P. (1982). The role of the father in gender identity, urethral erotism, and phallic narcissism. In S. H. Cath, A. R. Gurwitt, and J. M. Ross (Eds.), *Father and child. Developmental and clinical perspectives* (pp.175-187). Boston: Little, Brown and Company.

Vargo, M. E. (1998). *Acts of disclosure: The coming-out process of contemporary gay men.* Binghamton, NY: Harrington Park Press.

Voeller, B. and Walters, J. (1978). Gay fathers. *The Family Coordinator, 27*(2), 149-157.

Warren, C. (1980). Homosexuality and stigma. In J. Marmor (Ed.), *Homosexual behavior: A modern reappraisal* (pp. 123-141). New York: Basic Books, Inc.

Weeks, R. B., Derdeyn, A. P., and Langman, M. (1975). Two cases of children of homosexuals. *Child Psychiatry and Human Development, 6*(1), 26-32.

Weinberg, G. (1973). *Society and the healthy homosexual.* Garden City, NY: Anchor Books.

Weinstein, D. (2001). It's a radical thing: A conversation with April Martin, PhD. In D. F. Glazer and J. Drescher (Eds.), *Gay and lesbian parenting* (pp. 63-73). Binghamton, NY: The Haworth Press.

Wilde, O. (1888/1991). *The selfish giant.* New York: Scholastic Inc.

Willhoite, M. (1991). *Daddy's roommate.* Boston: Alyson Wonderland.

Williams, M. (1922/1991). *The velveteen rabbit or how toys become real.* New York: Doubleday.

Winnicott, D. W. (1960/1965). Ego distortion in terms of true and false self. In M. M. R. Khan (Ed.), *The maturational processes and the facilitating environment* (pp. 140-152). New York: International Universities Press, Inc.

Wolfenstein, M. (1966). How is mourning possible? *The Psychoanalytic Study of the Child, 21,* 93-123.

Woog, D. (1999). A collage of children: Stefan Lynch. In *Friends and family: True stories of gay America's straight allies* (pp. 72-81). Los Angeles: Alyson Books.

Wordsworth, W. (1913). Ode: Intimations of immortality from recollections of early childhood. *Selected poems of William Wordsworth* (pp. 461-466). London: Oxford University Press.

Index

Abelin, E. L., 17, 18
Absolute Gift, An (Rorem), *ix*
Abusive, 149
Acceptance, 36
    levels of, 145-147
    narcissistic, 145
    resigned, 145, 146
    unconditional, 145-146
        and the political climate, 155
Adjustment, 35
Adolescence, 21, 35
Age, and managing exposure of
        parent's homosexuality, 34
AIDS, 52
    as a loss, 36, 46, 69-72, 133, 138,
        155
Aleck, J., 42
All My Sons (Miller), 17, 25-26
Allen, D., 3
American Beauty (Cohen, Jinks, and
        Mendes), 39-41
American Family, An (Galluccio,
        Galluccio, and Groff), 4-6
Anality, 20
Analysis of data, 61
Anderson, D., 36
Anderson, S., 15
Androgyny/androgynous persona, 71,
    144
Anecdotal accounts
    by sons of gay fathers, 8, 46
    by/about gay fathers, 8
Anger, 33, 35, 36, 155
    in relation to being an Oedipal
        victor, 148
    in relation to betrayal/secrecy, 34,
        66, 71, 136
Arguelles, M. d. L., 3, 28, 53

Athena, 9, 13
Avoidant, 149

Bailey, J. M., 46
Baker, J. M., 31, 35, 36
Bargaining, 35
Barret, R. L., 3, 8, 45, 46, 50, 53
Baum, M. I., 27
Bear Dads, 51
Beeler, J., 151
Beginnings, 123-130
Benjamin, J., 18
Benkov, L., 28
Bergman, A., 17, 18
Bettelheim, B., 20
Bias, 58-59. *See also* Trustworthiness
    and impressions, 59-60
Bigner, J. J., 3, 7, 45
Bilsing, S., 41
Blos, P., 18, 21, 23, 150
Blumenfeld, W. J., 31
Bogdan, R., 54
Borhek, M. V., 36
Bornstein, B., 20
Boundary control, 33
Boy He Left Behind, The (Matousek),
    10-11
Bozett, F. W., 3, 7, 33, 45, 149
Brager, E. A., 8
Brammeier, S., 8
Brill, S. A., 8, 28, 45
Brown, A., 37
Buckner, R., 23
Buxton, A. P., *xiii, xvi, xviii*, 8, 27, 35,
    37, 38, 45, 46

Homosexuality. *See also* Gay, and its
relation to parenting style;
Gay father/parent; Gay
fatherhood/parenthood; Gay
son; Lesbian mother
as crisis, 8, 35
and Cuban culture, 70
and parenthood, 3
as stigma, 31, 66
*How Would You Feel If Your Dad Was
Gay?* (Heron and Maran), 27
Howey, N., 46
Huggins, S. L., 7
Hurt, 33
Hypocritical, 77, 103, 139, 149

Idealization
as a defense, 58, 149, 150
versus devaluation, 149
Identification, 18, 31, 58, 98, 149, 153
in relation to clinical practice, 156
Identity contamination, 34
Impact, 35, 138-144
Impulsive/Impulsivity, 91, 141, 149
In My Father's Arms (De Milly III),
44-45
In the Life, 46
Incest, 44-45. *See also* Gay father/parent,
as sexual abuser; Pederast;
Pedophile
Integration, 35
Intellectualization, 150
International Male, 76
Interview, 56-57. *See also* Interviewing;
Semistructured Interview
Guide
Interviewing. *See also* Interview;
Semistructured Interview
Guide
location of, 57
modes of, 57-58

"Intimations of Immortality from
Recollections of Early
Childhood" (Wordsworth),
145
Ira (the case of), 18-19

Jack (Homes), 1, 3, 34-35
Jack and the Beanstalk, 19-20
Jacobsen, R. B., 3, 7
Janus, 14
Jinks, D., 39
Johnson, L., 31
Jönsson, R., 16
Joyce, J., 16

Kafka, F., 15
Karslake, D., 3
Kaufman, G., 31
Keily, J., 42
Kid, The (Savage), 6
King, P., 11
Kirkpatrick, M., 7
Klein, F., 8, 45
Koff, B., 36
Kweskin, S. L., 7

Laius, 13
Langman, M., 3
Latency, 20
Leavitt, D., 43
Lesbian mother. *See also* Disclosure;
Gay father/parent; Gay
fatherhood/parenthood;
Mother; Son, adaptive
research on having a, 7
sons' stories highlighting a, 90, 91,
100, 103
Lesbian mother's partner, 90, 100
Letter to His Father (Kafka), 15
Levinson, R., 31
Lewis, K. G., 7

Symbiosis, 17
Symons, J., 46

Taylor, S. J., 54
Telemachus, 9, 12-13
That Certain Summer (Levinson, Link, and Johnson), 31-33
This is My Father (Clermont, King, and Quinn), 11-12
Thrasher, B. P., 20
Trustworthiness. *See also* Bias
 and member-checking, 54-56
 and use of an auditor, 54
Turner, P. H., 7, 53
Tyson, P., 18

Unlived Affections (Shannon), 39

Vargo, M. E., 46
Velveteen Father, The (Green), 6-7

Velveteen Rabbit, The (Williams), 7
Voeller, B., 3

Walters, J., 3
Warren, C., 31
Weeks, R. B., 3
Weinberg, G., 31
Weinstein, D., 3
What About the Children? (Saffron), 46
Whose Child Cries (Gantz), 29-30
Wilde, O., 1-3
Willhoite, M., 28
Williams, M., 7
Winnicott, D. W., 151
Wirth, A. G., 36
Wirth, M. J., 36
Wolfenstein, M., 21
Woog, D., 30, 46
Wordsworth, W., 145

Yearling, The (Rawlings), 21-23